Between the Stars and the Stones

Réjeanne Taylor
Calgary, Canada
2014

Between the Stars and the Stones

© Copyright 2014 Réjeanne Taylor

Printed in Canada

All rights reserved. No part of this publication may be reproduced, stored in or introduced into a retrieval system, or transmitted, in any form, or by any means (electronic, mechanical, photocopying, recording, or otherwise) without the prior written permission of the publisher. Requests for permission should be addressed to:
Robert Taylor, 1004A Lawrence Grassi Ridge,
Canmore AB T1W 3C2 Canada
or by e-mail to rwbobtaylor@shaw.ca

Taylor, Réjeanne   1948-2014
      Between the Stars and the Stones

ISBN: 978-1-312-77018-8

First printing in December 2014 by Lulu.com

Cover Photo: The author on the Via de la Plata, 2005

Dedication

(as it appeared in the original thesis)

To my mother, Ernestine (Guiffrey) Giasson,
A loving saint in heaven

&

To my father, François Xavier Giasson,
A faithful saint on earth.

Additional copies of this book may be purchased from:
www.lulu.com

All net proceeds from the sale of this book will be donated to Wellspring Calgary whose programs support people living with cancer.

http://wellspringcalgary.com/

Contents

Dedication iii

Forward 1

Introduction 3

Chapter 1: Longing 12

Chapter 2: Call 25

Chapter 3: Preparation 56

Chapter 4: Journey 85

Chapter 5: Arrival & Return 109

Chapter 6: Blessings 116

About the Author 127

Resources 129

End Note 130

The Little Company of Pilgrims of the Way of St. James - Canada presents this Pilgrim's Credential to

Full name __Réjeanne M. Taylor__
Street address __5108 Varscliff Road NW__
City __CALGARY__ Province __ALBERTA__
Passport number __VC 878186__ Emergency telephone __403-424-1411 (H)__
__403-423-9473 (Co)__
Medical conditions __NONE__

who began making his/her pilgrimage to Santiago de Compostela departing from __St. Jean Pied de Port__ on the __29__ of __Aug.__, 19__97__, by foot __X__, bicycle ____ horse back ____.

Completion of the Pilgrimage

27 SET. 1997

Santiago, a _____ de _____ de 19___

Forward

Between the Stars and the Stones is a love story. It is a story that reflects Réjeanne Taylor's passionate love of life, her love of family and her love for me. It also is a testimony to Réjeanne's deep and profound spirituality – grounded in the Christian tradition but reaching openly and with love to others, guided by God's grace.

This is a book that has evolved over seventeen years, beginning with her planning of our September 1997 family trip to Spain to walk 500 kilometres of the *Camino de Santiago*, a route traced by millions of feet over the last millennium. While I stepped off the train in Saint Jean Pied de Port with great uncertainty and trepidation about what was to befall our family of five, I walked secure in the credit cards tucked in my money belt and potential solutions they might provide. Réjeanne, however, stepped forth confident in the adventure that was to greet us, following uncertain paths with only the most limited knowledge of the Spanish language.

As Réjeanne relates in the pages that follow, this pilgrimage was fast-followed in December 1998 with the first steps of her pilgrimage with breast cancer; a pilgrimage not chosen but faced with a similar brave heart.

The parallels of those journeys formed the basis for the original thesis[i] submitted while earning her Masters of Arts in Spirituality and Worship Arts. In crafting this thesis, it was always Réjeanne's goal that this work be published in a non-academic setting and be available to a broad audience.

However, because that first cancer journey was "only a mastectomy" and had not involved either chemotherapy or radiation (and the attendant side effects), Réjeanne had self-doubts about the "legitimacy" of that journey as the basis for reaching out more broadly.

Those doubts were washed away in 2007 when breast cancer reappeared in the lymph nodes of that same side – but successfully treated with the "full meal deal" of chemotherapy, surgery and radiation. In what might be considered "typical Réjeanne fashion", she committed to walking daily no matter the weather [including snow and -25°C], with a goal of undertaking a virtual 800 km pilgrimage to Santiago using the pathways around our home. By the time treatment was finished, she had not only completed the 800 km Camino Francès but also the 1000 km Via de la Plata (which we had walked in Spain in 2005) – 1876 km in total!

Over the intervening years the original thesis has been re-worked and edited and was nearing completion when Réjeanne was once-again challenged in 2012 by a new and different breast cancer on the "other side". And once again she underwent the full regimen of chemo, surgery and radiation with a hopeful outcome.

But those hopes were dashed in the spring of 2014 when she was diagnosed once more with breast cancer; this time metastasized with "cure" not being within the oncologist's vocabulary. Réjeanne faced her final months with courage, humility and a certainty in the grace that would accompany her "final journey", and leaving behind the manuscript that appears in this book.

With one small exception, the words in this book are hers, that one exception being the "end of trip" emotions that we both shared and discussed. All of the photographs were taken by either Réjeanne or me.

The book title also evolved from its academic tone to *Between the Stars and the Stones*. The "stars" are the Milky Way -- considered by pilgrims to be synonymous with the Camino or Way of St. James; the "stones" refer to the blister inducing paths traversed on the way to Santiago. The title also reflects the realities of life's other tough journeys – the space we tread between our hopes and dreams and the tough realities that all too frequently confront us.

The final editing of this book and formatting it for publication has been Réjeanne's ongoing gift to me, as it has allowed me to re-visit and re-live these life-changing experiences. It is my hope that it has a similarly profound impact on you, the readers, and that Réjeanne's words (and her pilgrimage model) may help in some small way in whatever tough journeys enter your life.

        Ultreya,
        R.W. (Bob) Taylor

Introduction

Pilgrims, past and present, at the highest point of the Sierra del Perdón
(Taylor Family – 03 September 1997)

The idea of pilgrimage is much older than Christianity, but always it has been an expression of the same two main concepts: that of making a pilgrimage by travelling to a specific geographical site and that of being on a perpetual pilgrimage; the journey is life itself. Both are the pursuit of a greater good than mere existence, and both involve discomfort and hardship, if not a much overworked word, peril.

- Margaret Pawley, *Prayers for Pilgrims*[ii]

Annunciation

29 August 1997
A life-changing journey begins
The pilgrimage to Santiago de Compostela

> Deliberate
> Desired

An ancient pilgrimage
  brimming with
Anticipation, excitement, intention, perseverance, wholeness
  overflowing with

  Suffering
  Choice
  Blessing

28 November 1998
A life-changing journey begins
The pilgrimage with cancer

  Unsolicited
  Unwanted

A rampant disease
  swarming with
Anxiety, terror, fate, helplessness, infirmity
  overflowing with

  Suffering
  Choice
  Blessing

Réjeanne Taylor, April 1999

Introduction

two journeys

My full immersion in the process of pilgrimage began on August 29th 1997. On that ominous day, I excitedly set foot on a thousand-year old pilgrimage route that weaves across northern Spain from the French-Spanish border in the east to the shrine of St. James in the ancient town of *Santiago de Compostela* in the west. This pilgrimage is formally known as the Pilgrimage to *Santiago de Compostela* and affectionately referred to as the *Camino de Santiago* – the road of St. James. During this four-week journey, I walked five hundred and fifty exhilarating kilometres carrying everything I needed in a much too large backpack.

Exactly fifteen months later, November 28th 1998, I took my first tentative steps on another journey – a journey that I neither chose nor ever dreamt of undertaking – my first pilgrimage with breast cancer. This second journey came crashing through my well-ordered life and abruptly propelled me from a place of seeming invincibility to a terrifying place of foreboding where I had to face my own vulnerability … my own mortality.

How radically different could two journeys be?

At first, I could see only sharp contrasts between my journeys. The pilgrimage to *Santiago* was willingly chosen and full of experiences that are deemed to be life-enhancing: independence, physical endurance, achievement, community. The journey with breast cancer was unsolicited and replete with experiences that are usually considered life-eroding: dependence, physical ill health, disappointment, isolation.

But as my journey with breast cancer painstakingly unfolded, I began to recognize that this second journey encompassed many of the same characteristics as my geographical pilgrimage to *Santiago*. Both journeys focused for me a single purpose: safe arrival at the Cathedral of *Santiago* for the first journey, physical survival for the other. Both served to spotlight what is truly important and sacred in life. Both required thorough preparation. Both demanded determined physical and psychological effort. Both necessitated the surrender of the usual conditions of routine and control. Both encompassed a mysterious mixture of suffering, choice, and blessings.

I also became aware that in addition to exhibiting many of the same characteristics, my two journeys displayed an intriguing interaction. The walking pilgrimage informed my journey with cancer. The journey with cancer, in turn, further enlightened my earlier long distance trek on the *Camino de Santiago*.

Following my diagnosis, I frequently found myself drawn to the earlier experience of the walking pilgrimage in Spain to find solace and understanding for the journey with cancer. One day as I struggled to pray in the midst of my emotional upheaval and fear, I found great comfort in my pilgrimage journal entry dated the nineteenth of September 1997:

> *Visited the simple, ancient church of Santa Maria la Real in the mountaintop hamlet of O'Cebreiro. It is a pre-Romanesque structure of a kind typical of the area with a three-aisled interior and a rectangular apse. The simplicity of this church was very pleasing, after seeing so many overly ornate churches. While in the church, I*

Introduction

became aware of the gentle sound of rain and was instantly drawn, almost forcibly, to what was happening outside. I will never forget the scene through the tiny doorway of the small, ancient church. Outside – nurturing, evolving, moist, life. God's creation experiencing what God's creation has experienced since time began. Inside – cold, inanimate, gray, stone.

Looking out at wet flagstones from the doorway of Santa Maria la Real, O Cebreiro

And now here I was, fifteen months later, peering once again through the tiniest of doorways – straining for a glimpse of the life I knew before cancer became my terrifying reality. My earlier experience in the small church of *Santa Maria la Real* served to reassure me. Just as I had walked out of the cold, stone church into the fresh, moist air of the *Caurel / Ancares* mountains, I would one day walk out of my cold prison of fear into a world imbued with familiar color and promise. As my son so aptly predicted "Mom, your life will never be the same but you will get your life back."

In turn, my experience with cancer afforded me new perspectives on what I had discovered on the road to *Santiago*. Following my return from Spain I often mused about why this 550 kilometre walking pilgrimage had been such a profound, enriching experience. I knew some of the reasons: altered sense of time and distance, camaraderie with other pilgrims, ardent awareness of nature, daily engagement with medieval history, and mystifying rapport with those who had trod this path over the centuries. But somehow I knew that there was more to learn about this incredible journey.

My journey with cancer provided some further insight. The moment I learned that I might have cancer, the importance of life disentangled itself from the melee of pressing day-to-day distractions. In an instant, I became singularly focused. All that mattered was survival – doing everything I could to assure that I would continue to live, and living the life I did have as fully as possible. This alarming encounter with the possibility of death woke me from my sluggish slumber and I began again, like a small child, to pay attention to the little things in life.

I understood with greater clarity the counsel of Vietnamese monk Thich Nhat Hahnh: "The purpose [of life] is to be in the present moment and enjoy each step you make. Therefore you have to shake off all worries and anxieties, not thinking of the future, not thinking of the past, just enjoying the present moment."[iii]

Now, when I shared a hug with my husband or with my adult children, I gave myself more fully to the experience. No more hugs in passing – in a hurry to get to the next important distraction. I now hugged with presence

Introduction

and with full intent. Hugs were important moments to be lived and I lingered in my loved ones arms, absorbing the love, care, support, and energy carried in this simple human gesture.

Deer in yard of Varscliff Road Home

I also saw things with more wonder and appreciation. Two and a half weeks prior to surgery, Boxing Day 1998, I responded with renewed interest to the presence of four mule deer in our back yard. These deer are always a special sight since we live in a thirty-year-old urban neighbourhood and they wander up from the river only a few times each winter. But on this day, they were not only a source of delight; they were a source of reassurance and calm. I appreciated for the first time the deep serenity of these graceful creatures and their ability to simply *be*: comfortable in their skins, comfortable in their environment, comfortable in their circumstances. As I watched them that day, I was drawn into their calm – for a short time free of the foreboding that had enveloped me since the diagnosis of cancer.

My heightened awareness of these everyday moments added another piece to my understanding of why the pilgrimage to *Santiago* constituted such a transformative experience. Like my illness, the walking pilgrimage of twenty-nine days and five hundred and fifty kilometres had temporarily stripped away the many distractions of everyday life and freed me to attend to life's precious moments. During those weeks of walking across the ever-changing topography of northern Spain, I was "passionately present" to life as reflected in my journal entry dated 1 September 1997:

> *Walked another twenty kilometres today. The periodic rain added to the sense that we are now full-fledged peregrinos (pilgrims). Once again, we savoured a continuous display of gentle pastoral scenes. The area alongside a small meandering river was particularly breathtaking. As I filled my lungs with the warm, moist air I thought of the luscious rainforests of Vancouver Island. I marvelled at the density of the English Ivy that spread across the valley floor and crept up and around the tree trunks in heaven-bound spirals that finally disappeared from view under a canopy of thick branches.*

The frequent interplay between my walking pilgrimage to *Santiago* and my health journey with breast cancer continued during the weeks leading up to and following surgery. Through that interplay, I received the insights I needed to better understand, to slowly begin to accept, and to more fully engage my journey with illness. I also began to realize that my journey with cancer was also a pilgrimage – a genuine pilgrimage that encompassed the six universal phases of pilgrimage[iv] that I had already experienced on my pilgrimage to *Santiago*: Longing, Call, Preparation, Journey, Arrival, and Blessings.

Between The Stars and The Stones is an invitation to go on pilgrimage – to *Santiago*, and on any other difficult journey of transition, loss, illness

Introduction

or, in some circumstances, growth. It is an invitation to trust the road, to persevere through hardship, to celebrate even the seemingly everyday moments to share with others, to delight, and to give thanks. My hope is that with every kilometre you traverse, with every challenge you confront – you receive exactly what you need to engage your unique journeys, particularly the tough ones.

Réjeanne Taylor (March 2000)

Chapter 1: Longing
Anticipation - Anxiety

Catedral de Leon (Santa Maria de Regla)

How lovely are your dwellings, O God,
  how beautiful are the holy places.
In the days of my pilgrimage I yearn for them:
  they are the temples of your living presence.
I desire with longing to enter my true home:
  my whole being rejoices in the living God.
I thirst for the presence of the Holy in my life!

Jim Cotter, *Prayer at Day's Dawning*[v]

> *I thirst for the presence of the Holy in my life!*

What drew me to undertake the walking pilgrimage to Santiago de Compostela in northern Spain, my motivation for considering such an endeavour, was anything but clear. At first I did not know why. I only knew that I had to undertake this particular pilgrimage.

I did not realize until much later that I was responding to an unrelenting, persistent sense of longing. It was not until much later that I realized that my decision was a direct response to the passing of my eighty-year-old mother who had died a year earlier. I was still adjusting to the painful freedom of life without the security and nurture of my mother's unconditional love and understanding. I had also entered the stage of motherhood where I looked across the table one morning and saw, as if for the first time, three independent adults instead of three dependent children. My life, previously anchored by the rewards, demands and gifts of motherhood and daughterhood, was suddenly set adrift on an unknown sea of new expectations and new possibilities.

In addition to the sense of longing precipitated by shifts in life roles, I was also caught up in another incessant longing common to mid-life: the ever-growing quest for a deeper and deeper spiritual awareness. Although I had been raised in the Christian tradition and had been influenced by many genuine believers, I felt that my experience and knowledge of the Holy remained limited. I desperately wanted to explore the possibility that the God in whom I believed was infinitely greater, more loving, and more powerful than I could ever imagine. The following entries excerpted from my rather intermittent spiritual journal, express my profound longing for a more intimate, more dynamic relationship with God:

July 10th '95   *I thirst for the presence of the Holy in my life!*

January 8th '96   *My capacity for love is very limited. I want to be filled with the spirit of the Holy.*

October 5th '96   *Dear God, I want to love you more deeply!*

Given the shift in my roles as mother and daughter and my quest for a deeper spirituality, I was unmistakably moving from one life stage to another, experiencing the uncertainties and fears inherent to all life transitions. One moment I was energized with the anticipation of something new and exciting on the horizon; the next moment I was trembling with anxiety at what the future might hold. In spite of my apprehension about the future, I knew that I could not go back to what was and I could not remain in the present state of constant upheaval. I had to once again find my personal sense of purpose and direction in the world. I had no choice but to respond to the powerful sense of longing that was

Forested track in Galicia

drawing me forward. Like millions of other people over the course of history my response to this irresistible spiritual longing was to willingly embark on an arduous walking pilgrimage. On 29 August 1997, I took my first steps on the road that leads to Santiago and became, unbeknownst to me, what Martin Robinson refers to as a "hopeful traveller [who] seeks to meet with the holy as a means of bringing meaning to this life".[vi]

A mere fifteen months after taking those firsts step on the road to Santiago, I took my first tentative steps on a journey that I neither chose nor ever dreamt of undertaking.

This unsolicited journey began in November 1998 during the process of follow-up mammography. Six months earlier, suspicious changes in breast tissue had warranted a core biopsy that identified no malignancy but certainly indicated a need for close vigilance. Now, a brief six months later, x-ray images reflected additional changes that necessitated further exploration. An open biopsy was scheduled for December 8th. At the age of fifty, I was forced into a monumental life transition that I had not expected – certainly not at this relatively young age. I was abruptly propelled from a position of seeming invincibility and illusory immortality into a terrifyingly precipitous place where I had to face my own vulnerability ... my own mortality ... my own death.

Without intent, I found myself on another life-changing journey. But unlike the pilgrimage to Santiago, this second journey was not a response to an incessant longing. It was the unavoidable result of a serious health threat. Yet it too was replete with longing; longing unleashed by the threat itself. This longing - a longing for life, for health, for survival - was even more profound than the longing that had precipitated the pilgrimage to Santiago. Travel author Phil Cousineau, explains that the presence of an enduring, profound sense of longing is always the distinguishing factor between pilgrimage and other forms of journey. "What makes a pilgrimage ..... is the longing behind the journey".[vii]

Intrigued by the suggestion that my journey with illness was a pilgrimage, I was soon able to appreciate that the deep sense of longing at the heart of both journeys was actually an overwhelming desire to live – a desire to live longer, to live more intentionally, to live more passionately. I identified fully with Henry David Thoreau and his quest to live more than a fraction of life's potential. In *Walden,* his record of another kind of inwardly directed pilgrimage, Thoreau explains why he was drawn to the woods:

I went to the woods because I wished to live deliberately, to front only the essential facts of life, and see if I could not learn what it had to teach, and not, when I came to die, discover that I had not lived.[viii]

.. along the N-VI

Thoreau's explanation for his pilgrimage at Walden Pond reflected my own motivation when embarking on my two journeys. I too went on the pilgrimage to Santiago because I wished to live deliberately. And I reluctantly went on the pilgrimage with breast cancer not so much wanting to live more deliberately but desperately wanting to live…….

> *…a pilgrim will risk everything to get back in touch with life.*

Prior to embarking on the pilgrimage to the shrine of St. James in Santiago, I did not consider myself a long-distance backpacker. Although I was an avid hiker, I was only familiar with the relatively modest weight of an average daypack and had rarely hiked long distances for more than two days in a row. Now here I was, at the supposedly mature age of 49, strapping a 27-pound pack on my back (1/4 of my total body weight), with the declared aim of walking an average of twenty kilometres per day for an entire month. I was deliberately undertaking a journey that was challenging and rigorous, blatantly ignoring moderating considerations such as age, physical ability, and precedent. In the past, such considerations often would have constrained me from taking risks and attempting new adventures. If, as Cousineau maintains, "One of the ancient functions of pilgrimage is to wake us from our slumber",[ix] my decision to undertake the pilgrimage to Santiago awoke in me a sense of anticipation and excitement that could not be deterred or diluted. Born out of a longing for renewed meaning, mine was a pure passion that drove my vision forward with no regard for the stultifying cautions that often put to sleep great intentions mere moments after their inception.

Like pilgrimage, life-threatening illnesses also serve to wake us from our complacent slumber. Recently, a friend and business associate who has surrendered a lung to cancer, affirmed that as a result of his awakening, he never lets a day go by without expressing his love to his spouse and children. Another friend, an enthusiastic and creative school principal, explained how the many priorities of life dissolved into a single purpose, survival, the moment she discovered that she might have breast cancer. Both the process and result of a similar awakening has been documented, visually and poetically, by Stephanie Byram, an athletic young woman who had bilateral mastectomies shortly after her thirtieth birthday. Byram, with the help of photographer and friend, Charlee Brodsky, has created an inspiring web site photo essay entitled, *Cancer Destroys, Cancer Builds*. Byram forcefully expresses her radical awakening in one powerful sentence:

> *Cancer opened*
> *my mind, my eyes,*
> *my nose,*
> *my body, my sex*
> *my soul.*[x]

As in Stephanie's journey, the possibility of malignant breast cancer awoke in me an overwhelming greed for life. Once my life was threatened, I realized that I would do absolutely anything to ensure my survival. I would agree to any recommended form of intervention and treatment. I would modify my diet, my thoughts, my overall fitness. I would meditate, pray, and even plead with God. Life was too precious to leave any avenue of healing unexplored. I had never before experienced such an undeniable, unquenchable yearning for life. I was an impassioned pilgrim as described by Cousineau, "When life has lost its meaning, a pilgrim will risk everything to get back in touch with life".[xi]

Longing

This irrepressible human desire for life is, according to my friend and fellow cancer initiate[xii] Dat Nguyen, related to our origin in the Garden of Eden. Dat argues that in the Garden of Eden, prior to humankind's fall into forgetfulness, there was only life, healthy abundant life where illness and death were not known. Given humankind's earliest experience of everlasting life, he believes that somewhere in our collective subconscious we know unequivocally that life is eternal, without end. It is this knowledge or longing that pre-disposes us to reject physical death and to continue to grab hold of our earthly life in all circumstances, even in conditions replete with fear, hunger, pain, torture, hopelessness.[xiii]

Although Dat's thoughts affirmed my intense greed for life and offered a hopeful explanation for its existence, I discovered that the more I awoke to life the more perplexed I became regarding my own mortality. As a theist, I believe in eternal life but for obvious reasons I did not want to test that belief. I found it terrifying to think of leaving a mortal life that was known for an immortal life that was unknown and perhaps, just perhaps, only the imaginings of poets, artists, and mystics. Jazz artist, Louise Rose, poignantly captures this dilemma in her song "Nobody Wants To Sing The Blues."

> *Everybody wants to laugh*
> *Nobody wants to cry*
> *Everybody wants to go to heaven*
> *But nobody wants to die.*[xiv]

As my anxiety over the possibility of having breast cancer and my yearning for life both increased, I slowly began to understand that my hunger for life and my acceptance of my own mortality were not antithetical to one other. The acceptance of one was actually the condition necessary to give rise to the other. I attempted to explain this to myself in several journal entries:

***February 5th '99**   Today a friend pointed out that until we earnestly acknowledge our own mortality, we cannot live intently in the present. True faith is about uncompromising presence to the life we have been given. It is an unwillingness to forfeit any part of that life to regret, worry, guilt, denial, or complacency. When we remember who we are, the sons and daughters of God, we can live passionately and creatively because we know our lives have meaning and our destinies are eternal.*[xv]

***March 9th '99**   Like holy places, life-threatening illnesses are also holy ground because the terror they elicit is also about approaching the sacred. Breast cancer, like all other life-threatening illnesses, forces us to confront that horrifying end point – our own death. And what is death but that cross-roads where we finally come face to face with the holy – the God of all ages and of all peoples. As spiritual leaders have always taught, earthly death is not about the ultimate end but it is about the ultimate beginning. With death comes eternity – participation in the ongoing life of the sacred! The theory is that with this understanding we need no longer fear death and we can concentrate all our energies on living each precious moment!*

Easier said than done!

The more I pondered these journal entries and the problem they addressed, the more I understood that the desire to go on pilgrimage to a sacred site and the reality of a pilgrimage with a life-threatening illness are both invitations to life – thriving, exuberant, abundant life. I also realized that to be abundant, life cannot be limited to experiences of joy, achievement, confidence, calm, and peace. To be profusely abundant, life has to embrace sorrow, uncertainty, physical discomfort, monotony, fear, and the myriad of other less coveted experiences that make up the fabric of life.

Furthermore, these undesirable experiences must be embraced, not merely as interruptions of what would otherwise be an idyllic life, but as vital, integral elements of a life that embodies the wealth of human experience. Mystic and Carmelite monk, William McNamara, believes that a person who lives life with passion has "the ability to feel life in all its depth, in joy as well as in sorrow" and that the truly passionate amongst us "are those champions of mankind who are willing to sense life in its total polarity".[xvi]

When I first began to consider the nature of my two pilgrimages I was convinced that each of them represented some of the ultimate polarities of life. The chosen pilgrimage to Santiago embraced those life experiences that we consider to be life-giving and life-enhancing: freedom of choice, physical endurance, achievement, inspiration, and community. The unwanted pilgrimage with breast cancer, on the other hand, overflowed with experiences of life that we regard as life-eroding and life-destroying: lack of choice, physical ill-health, resignation, depression, and isolation.

> *... these two journeys were not as irreconcilable as I first thought*

The more I gazed at these two journeys, however, the more I began to see that they were not as irreconcilable as I first thought. Each journey contained within itself a host of life's polarities and these polarities did not remain ensconced in place but frequently gave way to their opposites. For example, on both pilgrimages I moved in and out of experiences of discomfort and comfort. On the walking pilgrimage to Santiago, foot pain was a constant companion. Each day I savoured the periods of rest when I could take the weight off my feet, release them from their leather bondage, and massage life and health back into them. On my health pilgrimage I remember vividly the initial discomfort of the cold operating theatres followed by the soothing comfort of warm blankets gently wrapped around my shivering body.

Further reflection suggested to me that my journeys were perhaps not made up so much of contradictory polarities but of complementary opposites that when embraced as a whole represented the fullness of powerful life experiences. My experiences of discomfort could not exist alone. One cannot know discomfort if one has not known comfort; one cannot know comfort if one has not known discomfort. We tend to define human experience in relation to its polarities. And so it is with all experiences: scarcity and abundance, anxiety and serenity, indifference and passion, safety and risk, invincibility and vulnerability, naïveté and wisdom, innocence and maturity, discouragement and hope.

It was becoming clearer and clearer to me that both of my journeys invited me to experience life in all its fullness and in all its mystery. Accepting this viewpoint with respect to the pilgrimage to Santiago was easy; accepting the same viewpoint with respect to the pilgrimage with breast cancer was infinitely more difficult.

Our society does not view journeys with life-threatening illnesses as life enhancing. Any journey involving suffering is seen as a negative, life eroding experience that must be tolerated but need not be embraced or celebrated. Society defines life experiences categorically and finitely: some experiences are good and worth living with passion and zest; others are bad, unwanted interruptions to passionate living, and worthy only of an attitude of resignation until life once again offers what is good and worthy of our full attention.

When I consider the photo documentation of my two pilgrimages I can see how fully I had adopted this good/bad view of life experiences. Whereas I have hundreds of prints (black & white, and colour) and hundreds of colour transparencies of the pilgrimage to Santiago, I do not have a similar documentation of my pilgrimage with breast cancer. It never even occurred to me to record the many salient, poignant moments of that journey: the walk to surgery that was really the walk towards the miracle of healing, the tender countenance of my loving husband whose constant presence during my hospital stay brought comfort and peace, the lively visits from our chaplain friend who regaled us with his humour and theological insights, the tentative visits from my adult children who strove to appear strong amid their private fears. This was life, worthy of full participation and documentation. This was life, worthy of being lived and not merely endured. And yet...?

As I pondered this dichotomy of response, I found clarification in the wisdom of the yogi master Paramahansa Yogananda, as paraphrased by Judith Cornell:

> According to Yogananda and all great masters, humankind's greatest goal is to overcome the cosmic illusion that all forms are separate and distinct: to rise above the laws of polarities that give us day and night, death and life, good and evil, pleasure and pain, light and shadow, and to experience ourselves and the universe as the totality of God's Absolute Nature – the One, illumined throughout by cosmic light.[xvii]

It was now abundantly clear to me that the relentless longing that I experienced at the inception of both the pilgrimage to Santiago and the pilgrimage with breast cancer was an invitation to intentional, participatory, abundant living. My only decision with respect to the first journey was whether or not I would respond to the invitation heralded by longing and actually embark on the pilgrimage that captured my imagination, my energy, my passion. Since an illness does not offer such a choice, my only decision with respect to the second pilgrimage was *how* I would respond to the invitation that had come crashing through my well-planned, well-ordered, healthy life.

Chapter 2: Call
Excitement – Terror

Trail leading down from Sierra del Perdón

I have called you by name; you are mine.

Isaiah 43:1

People return transformed

The first stirrings of a call to do the walking pilgrimage to Santiago de Compostela in northern Spain came to me as a total surprise and by the humblest of means. It was a lazy Saturday morning in early spring 1996. My husband and I had decided to indulge in a second cup of coffee and some leisurely reading from the selection of periodicals that had arrived that month. My selection was the April issue of Reader's Digest where my attention was drawn to a brief article on a thousand-year old pilgrimage route – the way of St. James – fondly known by millions of former pilgrims as the *Camino de Santiago*. Up to this point, I had not known that this ancient pilgrimage even existed. Through Deborah Cowley's brief but captivating account, I was introduced to the history of the *Camino*, to its burgeoning usage, to its many enticements, and to the observation that the journey itself was as important, if not more important, than the actual arrival.

The pilgrimage to Santiago de Compostela originated in the early ninth century with the reported discovery of the remains of St. James the Apostle in north-western Spain. Legend explains that following his death, the body of the first martyred apostle was brought by boat to the shores of Galicia on the Atlantic coast and that the saint's remains were buried a short distance inland. In AD 814 a local hermit informed his bishop that a shower of stars had led him to discover the ancient burial site of *San Iago*. When news reached the Pope, Rome quickly recognized the religious, political, and economic possibilities of such a discovery and wasted no time in declaring an official pilgrimage to the site.

The pilgrimage to Santiago, as it became known, quickly grew in popularity and by the 12th and 13th centuries it rivalled the more ancient pilgrimages to Jerusalem and Rome. At a time when the entire population of Europe was less than ten million, it is estimated that half a million pilgrims walked the route each year. These numbers are even more amazing when one considers that to travel the *Camino* during the Middle Ages involved a high degree of sacrifice and risk. Medieval pilgrims headed for Santiago left their homes and travelled for a minimum of three months and up to several years, endured countless privations, suffered frequent illness and injury, and risked possible beating and death at the hands of bandits. Pablo Arribas Briones suggests that such fervor was a result of the spiritual rewards to be gained by walking the pilgrimage route: "Those Christians felt certain that if they made the pilgrimage to Santiago or died trying, they were assured of reaching heaven."[xviii]

Old Roman road approaching Cirauqui

Since the Middle Ages, interest in the pilgrimage to Santiago has ebbed and flowed. In the early 1960s, a Spanish priest named Elías Valiña spearheaded a restoration and preservation project. Over the next ten years Elías and several associations known as the *Amigos del Camino de Santiago* researched the original route, restored the paths, marked the way with bright-yellow arrows, and began work on the re-establishment of adequate *refugios* or pilgrims' hostels.

Since then, there has been a growing resurgence of interest in the pilgrimage to Santiago. Each year tens of thousands of pilgrims from all corners of the world leave the safety and comfort of their homes to engage in this ancient form of spiritual and physical activity. Due primarily to time constraints, however, most of today's pilgrims do not begin their trek at the traditional French starting points of Paris, Vézelay, Le Puy, and Arles. Instead, most modern *peregrinos* begin at St. Jean Pied de Port, a small French town at the foot of the Pyrénées. From this point, the distance to Santiago de Compostela is roughly seven hundred and eighty kilometres: a distance that can be walked in three weeks by the fanatic/athletic few and in six weeks by most others. The seven hundred and eighty kilometre trail immediately climbs up the rugged Pyrénées, over the hills of Navarra, into the wine valleys of Rioja, across the vast plains of Castilla-León, over the alpine mountains of Galicia, and finally into the hallowed valley of Santiago.

Cowley recommends not hurrying across the *Camino* since there is so much to savour along the way: the breathtaking Spanish countryside, the intriguing styles of architecture, the massive cathedrals and monasteries, the fascinating myths, the remarkable interaction with fellow pilgrims, and the warm-hearted hospitality of the locals. Cowley cites the words of a priest and those of a former pilgrim to emphasize that the journey is as important, if not more important, than the actual arrival at Santiago. Don

José María Alonso, the kind priest who serves the small hamlet of San Juan de Ortega, has this to say about the importance of the journey itself, "There's a special magic along that road. It may be the silence or the scenery. Whatever it is, it's not the arriving at Santiago that's important; it's what happens along the way. People return transformed."[xix] Laurie Dennett, a woman who in 1986 walked 1,600 kilometres from the French city of Chartres to Santiago, attempts to explain how she was transformed:

> *By the time you finally walk down the aisle of that magnificent cathedral, you realize that your pilgrimage is about putting into practice all you have been given: all that trust, all the things you have learned about living and travelling with others. It begins on your way up the aisle, and it will last as long as you live.*[xx]

When I finally put down the Reader's Digest, after absorbing every last bit of information it offered on this fascinating pilgrimage, I was hooked. I could not remember another time in my life when I was so motivated or called to do one particular thing. The brief description of a pilgrimage so ancient and so far away grabbed my imagination with such force that I looked up at my husband, who was calmly and unsuspectingly reading <u>Outdoor Photographer</u>, and declared: "When we retire, we will do this pilgrimage." My words were definite, conclusive, unwavering. The firm resolve spoken that fateful day was translated into action a short sixteen months later.

On 29 August 1997, as part of our 25th anniversary celebration and long before retirement, we got off the train in St. Jean Pied de Port and placed our boot-clad feet on the ancient road to Santiago. Our backpacks were heavy and so were our hearts. Our backpacks bulged with what we considered the minimal necessities of life and our hearts pounded with anticipation, fear, excitement, and expectation. I had heard the demanding call to this particular pilgrimage and I had responded to that call with a resounding 'yes'; my husband and adult children who accompanied me were willing but unwitting companions.

Why was God calling me to this horrifying journey? My second journey, the journey with breast cancer, began as it does for many women, with a call to enter a small x-ray room for additional imaging of worrisome breast tissue. As briefly mentioned in Chapter 1, the resultant mammography indicated a need for an open biopsy that was performed on 8 December 1998, roughly fifteen months after taking my first steps on the Camino de Santiago. Within twenty-four hours of this exploratory surgery I received *the call* from the surgeon:

> *Réjeanne, the preliminary pathology report indicates that we are dealing with a pre-cancer condition known as Ductal Carcinoma in Situ. DCIS was prevalent throughout the biopsy specimen including*

the margins. That is, malignant cells were found at the cut surface of the excision biopsy. Since there is no clear margin, the most prudent course of action is likely a mastectomy, with or without reconstruction. I have scheduled our next meeting for a week from now. At that time, we will have the complete report from pathology and we can evaluate the situation further. Would you like to talk with me before then?

I was stunned. Although, like most women who undergo breast biopsies, I had considered the possibility of a mastectomy, the surgeon's words took the dreaded surgery from the realm of possibility to the domain of stark, inescapable reality – my reality. I had joined the growing sisterhood of women who are asked to surrender a soft, sensitive, nurturing, life-giving part of themselves in return for the harsh reality that this surrendering provides the best hope of survival.

A week later my husband, Bob, and I met with the surgeon, Dr. René Lafrenière, to review the now complete pathology findings. Bob continued to be my willing but unwitting companion on this journey too, as he had been throughout the hundreds of kilometres of the *Camino*. On the *Camino* he had served as patient backpack holder and lookout the myriad of times that I had to scoot off the trail to attend to nature's call. He had provided constant encouragement and helpful humour on many hot, exhausting days. He had tended to blisters and lovingly massaged tiger balm into my knotted but increasingly muscular calves.

On this frightening, life-threatening journey he was once again a steady source of patience, strength, encouragement and loving tenderness. He also functioned as an indispensable second listener and capable scribe. Throughout the many appointments and procedures involved in this second pilgrimage journey, I often found that I had to confirm with Bob what I thought I had heard or understood about my situation since my listening skills were often dulled by waves of panic and fear.

At my request, Dr. Lafrenière started our meeting by clarifying the term "pre-cancer". He explained that the term "pre-cancer" is used to differentiate cancer cells that are not yet invasive, from cancer cells that are invasive. The cells in question were indeed malignant but fortunately, to this point, these diseased cells had chosen to remain in their place of origin, hence the term, *in situ*. The concern was that these dangerous cells could decide at any time to break through the membrane that kept them localized and invade surrounding healthy tissue and beyond. He further explained that testing of the biopsied breast tissue indicated high-grade DCIS lesions. He added that studies to date showed that high-grade DCIS tumours had a greater probability of developing into invasive cancers than low-grade tumours. Given the particular nature of the DCIS, waiting to see if these cells would one day become invasive was a foolhardy alternative. The urgency of the situation became clearer and clearer to me as I struggled with a deluge of mixed emotions, ranging from sheer panic to rational assessment of the facts before me.

Over the period of a few short weeks, I had heard a terrifying ***Call*** – a call that, result by result, heralded a threat to my life. Without wishing or willing, dreaming or planning, I found myself inextricably placed on another journey, the pilgrimage with breast cancer. Like the pilgrimage to Santiago, this pilgrimage gripped my imagination with terrifying force.

Only this time, while I had given my whole-hearted assent to the fascination of Santiago, I vehemently rejected the advances of the pilgrimage with breast cancer. As we drove home from the surgeon's clinic that memorable day in mid-December, I pleaded with my husband through tears of horror and disbelief: "There must be some mistake! There is no history of breast cancer in my family! I exercise regularly and I eat a wholesome diet! How can this be?" My words were questioning, incredulous, denying.

The diagnosis of cancer propelled me into a cold, dark dimension of desperate isolation where it seemed that only I existed. In the following weeks, I strained against this numbing isolation but could not regain my solid footing in the world that I knew. I could only perceive that world from afar, as if seeing and hearing from a long, dank, narrow, echoing tunnel. From this desolate vantage point, the world that rushed before me appeared to be full of only healthy people, feverishly preparing for Christmas. Full of women, all of whom to all outward appearances, had two voluptuous, healthy breasts. Although intellectually I knew differently, emotionally I was sure that I was the only woman at this joyous time of the year who faced or had faced the traumatizing disfigurement of mastectomy. Why had I been singled out for special consideration? Why could I not remain part of the unnamed, uncalled, unaffected masses?

As I struggled to maintain some sort of equilibrium, the nagging question, "Why me?" started to hammer at my consciousness. During the five weeks preceding surgery, I frequently awoke in the middle of the night frightened, angry, and rampant with questions. How could this have happened? How could the breast that had nourished my babies and taught me so much about the depth and breadth of maternal love now be a threat to my life? How could a part of me that had brought my husband and me so much pleasure, love, tenderness, and ecstasy have become so menacing? How could a part of me that had, not so long ago, been so life giving now be poised to deal a deathblow? "What had gone wrong?" "Why was God doing this to me?" "What had I done?" "Why was God calling me to this horrifying journey?"

One morning, after yet another sleepless night's barrage of perplexing thoughts and haunting questions, I suddenly realized that the questions I was asking reflected my deep-seated beliefs about how the world worked and how suffering fit into that world. For example, I would not have asked, "Why was God doing this to me?" if I did not at some level still believe in an all-powerful God who determined and delivered suffering. I would not have asked, "What had I done?" if I did not believe that I was in some way responsible for my own suffering. And I would not have asked, "Why was God calling me to this horrifying journey?" if I did not believe that each of us has a special calling or destiny.

As I sat at my kitchen table that morning, I was shocked to discover that my worldview was still being influenced by images of a punitive and disciplinary God. I reviewed the three standard explanations construed by Judaeo-Christian theologians to reconcile their perception of God's abundant goodness with their belief that He also orchestrates suffering: God sends suffering to test our faith, God sends suffering as divine punishment, and God sends suffering in order to build our character. Although I could understand that these explanations were attempts to bring some sort of understanding to the issue of innocent suffering, I could not accept the God that such explanations revealed: a jealous, vindictive God. I also sensed that such explanations did not capture the breadth of who God is, nor the enormous complexity of our lives. I agreed wholeheartedly with authors Herbert Anderson and Edward Foley who wrote: "An authentic faith journey in all its paradoxical pain and wonder does not allow for facile resolution."[xxi]

In my desperate quest to discover what role God played, if any, in the onset of my illness I turned to the book of Job in the Hebrew Bible. Over the years I had often heard people say that in their darkest moments, whether due to serious illness or to the loss of a loved one or to a marriage break-up, they had found some solace in the unfortunate story of Job. My personal review of the book of Job was both disturbing and thought provoking. This book explores the nagging question of why there is innocent suffering in the world and focuses primarily on two of the common Judaeo-Christian explanations: suffering is sent by God to test our faith, and suffering is sent by God as punishment for our wickedness.

The explanation that suffering is sent by God to test our faith is introduced in the first chapter of the book of Job and is the starting point of Job's miseries. In that chapter, God gives Satan permission to test Job's loyalty. "Very well, then, everything he has is in your hands, but on the man himself do not lay a finger." Satan takes his task very seriously and proceeds to wipe out Job's sons, daughters, servants, sheep, camels, oxen, and donkeys. Now heartbroken and destitute, Job continues to be loyal to God and "does not sin by charging God with wrongdoing".[xxii]

Frustrated by Job's steadfast loyalty, Satan returns to God in Chapter 2 and asks permission to test Job further, convinced that painful sores over his entire body will drive Job to curse God to his face. Once again, we see God's willingness to allow Job to be tested, "Very well, then, he is in your hands; but you must spare his life".[xxiii]

I found the idea that God collaborated with Satan in testing Job, to be repugnant and antithetical to the nature of God. Surely, God is too magnanimous and too busy loving and caring for people and the earth to bother playing games with Satan, at the expense of unwary humans. I found the author's attempts to make Satan the agent of the suffering rather than God himself, to be a weak attempt at absolving God from responsibility. In courts of law, accomplices are deemed to be as guilty as the perpetrators of crimes. Similarly, in this "testing of faith" explanation of why Job had to suffer, God remains the prime mover since without his approval the testing of Job's loyalty would not have occurred. I again find this inconsistent with the God that I know. A loving God whose first goal is to protect His children – not to offer them up.

With respect to the explanation of suffering as divine punishment, Job and his would-be supporters engage in a lengthy, passionate war of words. Job's supporters insist that suffering is a result of divine punishment. Job argues that from his own desperate experience, suffering is not necessarily a result of divine punishment since suffering is unleashed on the righteous as well as the wicked. He repeatedly asserts his pure, sinless nature and argues that suffering is foisted on the innocent and righteous as often, if not more often, than on the wicked. Job's supporters cannot even begin to conceive of a world order that does not support a causal relationship between behaviour and suffering. They believe so strongly that suffering is only sent to those who have sinned that they adamantly reject Job's assertion of innocence. During one passionate discourse, Eliphaz, one of Job's supporters, lists the probable sins that Job must have committed to warrant such suffering at the hands of a just and righteous God:

> *Is not your wickedness great?*
> *Are not your sins endless?*
> *You demanded security from your brothers for no reason;*
> *You stripped men of their clothing, leaving them naked.*
> *You gave no water to the weary*
> *and you withheld food from the hungry,*
> *though you were a powerful man, owning land –*
> *an honoured man, living on it.*
> *And you sent widows away empty-handed*
> *and broke the strength of the fatherless.*
> *That is why snares are all around you,*
> *why sudden peril terrifies you,*
> *why it is so dark you cannot see,*
> *and why a flood of water covers you. (Job 22:5-11)*

As I read the lengthy elaboration of Job's agonizing experience, I found myself passionately rejecting his supporters' many reasoned arguments promoting the idea that God sends suffering as divine punishment. I knew that if I accepted this explanation of why there is innocent suffering in the world, I would have to accept that God was vindictive and cruel. The God in whom I believe, the God who was first revealed to me by loving parents and later by other family members and mentors, is a God of love, forgiveness, and compassion. I could never, especially at this time of emotional upheaval and uncertainty, abandon the security of a loving God for the vagaries of a vengeful, jealous deity.

After forty-two chapters of verbose speculation on the reasons for innocent suffering, all of which implicate God as judge, perpetrator, and sovereign ruler, the author of Job, in a brief epilogue, finally introduces God as forgiving, merciful, and generous but it is clearly too little too late. First impressions are lasting and extremely difficult to dislodge. By the time readers get to the epilogue, they have already been bombarded with the repeated explanations that God allows or sends suffering our way to test us or to punish us. In addition, we hear in Job's apologetic reply to God in the final chapter the suggestion of character building:

> *I know that you can do all things;*
> *no plan of yours can be thwarted.*
> *You asked, 'Who is this that obscures my counsel*
> *without knowledge?'*
> *Surely I spoke of things I did not understand,*
> *things too wonderful for me to know. (Job 42:2-3)*

When I finished reading this lengthy argument on suffering I was still left with the three standard explanations of suffering, none of which I could accept. Years earlier, I had already concluded through the suffering of friends and family that these explanations did not reflect the God in whom I believed. Now in the throes of my own anguish and anger I was even more opposed to such disciplinary explanations of suffering. I agreed whole-heartedly with religious philosopher, Brian Hebblethwaite, that all three explanations "cast grave doubts on the goodness of God." [xxiv] I recoiled at the slightest possibility that the call to a journey with breast cancer was the result of God's decision to test me, to punish me, or to build my character. I knew that the God I needed to walk with me through this illness was the God, also from my Judaeo-Christian tradition, who was forgiving, loving, and compassionate. That morning I resolved to resist the influence of any thought or question that suggested that God had sent me breast cancer for any supposedly righteous reason.

I was livid!

The importance of this resolve became evident in the ensuing weeks as I was confronted with some of the traditional explanations of suffering. No matter how often I sent these explanations to the emotional trash bin, some well-meaning soul retrieved them and held them up as valid justifications for what was happening to me. One day, I was outraged by the message on a beautiful greeting card that had been left in our mailbox. The message was clearly an adaptation of Zechariah 13:9, "… I will refine them like silver and test them like gold." Although God was not identified by name, the implication that God had sent this suffering my way so that I could learn and grow was anything but subtle. The card read:

> *Just like gold must be fired*
> *to expose its lustre*
> *And silver must be refined*
> *to create its value*
> *So too*
> *this difficult time*
> *will reveal the full potential*
> *of your inner self.*[xxv]

I was livid! This message could have only been more insensitive if it had included a third metaphor: And diamonds must be cut to reveal their beauty. How dare someone preach to me, especially via a greeting card, that this wretched breast cancer and the necessary mastectomy were good for my personal development! And what was wrong with the self that I had already worked fifty years to develop? As soon as I heard myself verbalize these reactions out loud, I felt guilty and ashamed at my response to the love offering of a friend who was, I had no doubt, sincerely trying to be supportive. How could I respond so selfishly to intended words of encouragement; words that were, I now sheepishly acknowledged, accompanied by a lovely box of chocolates?

The answer was obvious. First there was the suggestion that God had sent this difficult experience my way in order to build my character. How often would I have to refute this unpalatable explanation of suffering? Secondly, I deeply resented being told through a greeting card something that I already knew: adversity leads to personal growth. You cannot live fifty years on this earth and not know this obvious truth. But it was clearly too early for me to be able to embrace that truth with respect to my journey with breast cancer. My emotional outburst was both because God was implicated as the instigator of my suffering and because another person had taken it upon herself to tell me that my experience with breast cancer was ultimately good for me, long before I was ready to entertain that possibility.

Carol Matzkin Orsborn, co-author of *Speak the Language of Healing: Living with Breast Cancer without Going to War*, cautions well-meaning friends and family members not to theorize in any way about the reasons and associated benefits of another person's serious illness. Matzkin Orsborn advises that such speculation "comes off as patronizing at best."[xxvi] To this I responded "Yes!". Seeing the growth opportunities from an experience of suffering is up to the sufferer to determine, in her or his own time.

Later that week, in my continued quest to make sense of my experience with breast cancer, I began to read John Packo's account of his experience with cancer, *Coping With Cancer and Other Chronic or Life-Threatening Diseases*. I once again unwittingly came face to face with a God who deliberately sends suffering for supposedly righteous reasons. The third chapter of Packo's book is entitled, Creative Choice #3: "Since our sovereign Lord permits cancer for His glory and our spiritual growth, I will glorify God and grow."[xxvii] I could not help but wince at the phrase, "permits cancer for His glory". "Now that's an arrogant God!" I thought, as I closed the book and relegated it to the return pile.

My resolve to reject the explanations for suffering that held God responsible for my cancer, while it clarified and affirmed my understanding of who God is, did nothing to explain why I had breast cancer. If God was not responsible, then who or what was? In my desperate attempt to come up with an answer I turned my attention to the recurring question, "What had I done?" This question reflected my acceptance of the prevalent belief that those who suffer are ultimately responsible for their suffering.

Immediately following my diagnosis, I had picked up a copy of *Dr. Susan Love's Breast Book* to read more about my particular cancer, *Ductal*

Carcinoma In Situ. Now, I returned to the book, intent on finding a cause for my illness. The nagging need to know why this had happened fuelled my exploration. I could not tolerate the possibility that health and ill-health were just a matter of chance occurrence. That possibility frightened me because of its damning implication of utter powerlessness. I was fixated on finding a cause and effect explanation for my cancer in order to regain some sense of control. Even if I discovered that I was in some way responsible for my illness, the ensuing guilt would be worth it since I would finally understand why this had happened to me. I would also be better positioned to prevent it from happening again.

I began my search by reading Dr. Love's chapter on genetic and hormonal risk factors. These include family history, early menarche, late menopause, first child after thirty, and no pregnancies. [xxviii] I could not claim any one of these risk factors so I moved on to the chapter on external risk factors: diet, alcohol, radiation, birth control pills, fertility drugs, hormone replacement therapy, and environmental hazards. [xxix] Again, the majority of these risk factors did not apply to my situation. The two factors that did apply were diet and alcohol. I started to wonder if my propensity for sweets and desserts over the years and my enjoyment of the occasional glass of red wine were perhaps at the root of this illness. This feeble hint of responsibility quickly exploded into a barrage of self-recriminations. Why had I not read this information before? Why had I not taken better care of my breasts? Why had I not adopted a breast cancer prevention diet long before now?

As I winced under the load of fear, anger, and self-blame, my husband Bob once again offered calm. In his wonderful, clear-thinking way of looking at things, he assured me that I had done nothing to cause my breast cancer. He pointed out that diet, alcohol consumption, and all the other factors that I had considered as possible reasons for my breast cancer are identified as *known risk factors* associated with the development of breast cancer. They are not identified as *known causes* of breast cancer. He gently pointed back to two statements that I had underlined in Dr. Love's book.

> *It would be much more convenient if we could say, "This causes breast cancer so don't do it." But breast cancer ... is what is known as a "multifactorial disease" – that is, it has many causes which interact with each other in ways we don't understand yet.*[xxx]

> *In fact, 70 percent of breast cancer patients have none of the classical risk factors in their background.*[xxxi]

With these facts fresh in my mind, I released my self-inflicted feelings of guilt, regret, and self-recrimination. Since medical research could not offer any definitive causal connections between my lifestyle and the onset of my breast cancer I resolved to heed the importance of *known risk factors* but not to elevate them to the status of *known causes* with the associated implication of sure prevention.

In the relative moments of calm following these days of numbing intellectual aerobics, I realized that although my feelings had pushed me into and around my exploration of the "why" questions, I had depended solely on reason to probe these questions. I remembered that Evelyn Underhill, in her classic work *Mysticism*, asserts that understanding our experiences through our emotions is more important than understanding them through our intellects. I retrieved her book from the shelf and re-read her wise words:

> *It is a matter of experience that in our moments of deep emotion, transitory though they may be, we plunge deeper into the reality of things than we can hope to do in hours of the most brilliant argument. At the touch of passion doors fly open which logic has battered on in vain: for passion rouses to activity not merely the mind, but the whole vitality of man [sic]. It is the lover, the poet, the mourner, the convert, [the sufferer] who shares for a moment the mystic's privilege of lifting that Veil of Isis which science handles so helplessly, leaving only her dirty fingerprints behind.*[xxxii] *The heart, eager and restless, goes out into the unknown, and brings home, literally and actually, "fresh food for thought."*[xxxiii]

Underhill's words gave me renewed hope that I might yet be able to come to a palatable understanding of my situation, not through the intellectual evaluation of statistics and facts, but through a passionate participation in the life before me.

...the world will never be the same again.

As I opened up to new possibilities, my thoughts transported me back to San Juan de Ortega, a small wilderness hamlet on the Pilgrim's Road to Santiago. As I visualized that isolated hamlet of eight inhabitants, the large Romanesque pilgrims' church, (parts of which date back to the 12th century), and the small frame of Don José Maria Alonso, I was filled with an overwhelming sense of love and re-assurance. Don Alonso is the kind parish priest that I had first read about in Cowley's article and that I later had the privilege of meeting on my own Spanish pilgrimage. In the midst of all the confusion, anger, and terror around why I had breast cancer, the small hamlet in the middle of the Spanish wilderness loomed as an emotional safe-haven that offered consolation, comfort, and wellbeing.

Pilgrims of the Middle Ages also considered San Juan de Ortega to be a safe haven. When pilgrims saw the Church of St. Nicholas emerge through the trees they knew they had survived one of the most treacherous

Wilderness Monastery of San Juan de Ortega

stretches of the *Camino*. The desolate region of the Oca Mountains was a popular abode for thieves who lived off of the spoils of the steady stream of resolute pilgrims headed for the shrine of St. James. San Juan himself noted in his record of the year 1152 that thieves robbed and killed travelers day and night in the hills of the Oca Mountains.[xxxiv]

Many centuries later, without risking our lives to bandits, we had made our jubilant approach to San Juan de Ortega on the afternoon of 12

September 1997. As it had for previous generations of pilgrims, the church of St. Nicholas had suddenly risen above the trees, signaling that we had finally reached our day's destination where we knew we would be offered food, shelter, safety, and spiritual sustenance. Following the customary routine of claiming our sleeping space, taking a shower, washing our clothes, and enjoying a meal at the local bar, we had entered the peaceful sanctuary of St. Nicholas to attend evening mass. The sanctuary had been full of fellow pilgrims who, like Bob and I, reveled in the cool, restful interior of the stone church.

Following the mass, Don Alonso had offered some words of explanation with regards to the exquisitely carved triple capital in the northern apse of the church. Through interpretation provided by fellow pilgrims, we had learned that the sculpture that most captured Father Alonso's imagination was the figure of the young Virgin Mary, at the moment when she was called by the angel

Capital in Nave of Iglesia de San Nicolás, Monastery of San Juan de Ortega

Gabriel to be the mother of Jesus. Inspired by this image, Don Alonso had enthusiastically shared two insights with our tiny band of pilgrims. At the time, his convincing words had greatly encouraged our weary bodies and deeply stirred our restful hearts. Now, several months later, as I wrestled with my own special call, Don Alonso's wisdom once again filled my weary body with encouragement and my restless heart with a peaceful anticipation.

Realize that you are privileged to be on this particular pilgrimage and that the fact that you are here is not just a chance occurrence.

Be open to God during this special time because, just as it was for Mary, once you have been "illuminated" or "called" by the Holy Spirit, the world will never be the same again.

I remembered how easy it was for me to accept Don Alonso's words of wisdom with respect to the inspirational experience of the pilgrimage to Santiago. Of course I was privileged to be on that pilgrimage and I had no hesitation in accepting the idea that God had called me to that journey. I do not usually struggle with the question, "Why did this happen to me?" when I am the recipient of happy, meaningful experiences. For example, I never thought of asking, "Why me?" when I married my wonderful husband or when my three healthy babies were born. These I willingly accepted as part of my unique journey and praised God for her goodness.

Now here I was some fifteen months later, struggling to accept the reality of breast cancer as integral to my unique journey! I had a great deal of hesitation in accepting the idea that God had called me to this particular experience. But the more I reflected on Don Alonso's words the more I was drawn to them. I sensed their powerful wisdom. They were somehow prophetic and at some level I knew that they spoke as profoundly to my present pilgrimage with illness as they had to my walking the *Camino*. There was something in those words that I needed to understand. But still I hesitated. If I pursued their meaning further, would I again come face to face with the belief that God had sent breast cancer to test me, to punish me, or to build my character? As I hesitated, I thought of Don Alonso with his twinkling eyes, playful smile, and rock-solid faith, a faith that shone through linguistic and cultural barriers. This man could be trusted, I thought, and I opted to plunge deeper into the insights that he had lovingly shared. This time, however, I decided to accept Underhill's counsel: "In the sphere of religion it is now acknowledged that 'God known of the heart' gives a better account of the character of our spiritual experience than 'God guessed at by the brain'."[xxxv] I resolved to let my intuition have freer reign.

As I reflected on Don Alonso's first statement in the light of my present situation, I trembled in disbelief: *Realize that you are privileged to be on this particular pilgrimage* [with breast cancer] *and that the fact that you are here is not just a chance occurrence.* There it was again, the repugnant notion that this illness was good for me and that it was earmarked for me alone. Sensing my usual negative response to this view of suffering, I made a conscious effort to remain open to new understandings.

The moment I opened my mind and heart to new possibilities, I found Don Alonso's words strangely comforting. First, because they affirmed that my illness was not a chance occurrence, I could take comfort in the fact that there was, after all, some sort of order in the world. Second, because Don Alonso's words affirmed the meaning and value of my illness, I could take comfort in knowing that the fear, anger, pain, loss and anguish of this journey were not pointless. And third because these words implied that this journey with breast cancer was uniquely mine, I could take comfort in knowing that only I could walk this particular journey. In his poem, "The Call", Jules Supervielle aptly describes the sense of anticipation that I experienced when I let myself entertain the thought that I had a special role to fill in this life and that my illness was part of that role:

And it was then that in the depths of sleep
Someone breathed to me: "You alone can do it,
Come immediately."[xxxvi]

This characteristic of uniqueness stood in sharp contrast to a journey that, until now, offered only a dreaded, dehumanizing sameness: x-rays, biopsies, surgeries, treatments, examinations, records, hospital gowns, identification bracelets, intravenous poles, hospital meals.

With a burgeoning sense of wonder, I moved on to the first clause of Don Alonso's second statement: *Be open to God during this special time* [of illness]… Certainly, walking the *Camino* had been a special time. I had never before experienced such a significant altering of my sense of time and distance. I will never forget the moment that forced me into this abrupt realization.

It was the afternoon of our sixth day on the *Camino*. Under a blazing sun and in temperatures of 35°C, we had completed a twenty-four-kilometre trudge from Pamplona over the mountain ridge of Puerto del Perdón. We were so exhausted when we reached the attractive town of Puente la Reina that we decided to take a hotel for the night rather than bunk into the municipal *refugio* (hostel), well-known at the time[xxxvii] for its cramped quarters and shaky

Puenta la Reina

What a luxury it was to take showers and wash out our clothes in the spacious privacy of our own room! Before we left the hotel to find dinner, I approached the young lady at the reception desk and asked her where we could find a *mercado* or market. She smiled sweetly and explained that there was a small *mercado* in town but that if we wanted to shop at a *supermercado* there was one nearby in Pamplona.

I was stunned by her suggestion and almost jumped across the desk with the express purpose of beating some sense into her. How could she even think of suggesting that we go back to Pamplona? It had taken us an excruciating day of arduous physical effort to get here. In the next instant my brain cleared and I realized that this innocent young woman did not know that we had arrived on foot. She assumed that we, like most of her other guests, had a car parked just outside.

After thanking her profusely, I walked into the evening air, totally incredulous that a distance that could be covered in a mere fifteen minutes by car had taken us all day to walk. It was then that I realized to what extent my perception of time and distance had shifted since I first set foot on the *Camino*.

In a similar way, my walk with breast cancer was a special time of altered awareness of time and distance. Days of waiting for results that held my future in their threatening clutch seemed like interminable months. The short distance down clinic and hospital corridors seemed like miles of foreboding passageway. And waits of a few minutes in cheerless waiting rooms seemed like endless hours of fearful, agitated expectancy.

Upon further reflection I realized that my two journeys were special not so much because of the shift in time and distance but because of what those shifts in time and distance meant in terms of intensity of living.

Go out and walk in the rain!

For months after returning from Spain, my thoughts would, without the slightest warning, place me back on the *Camino*. While I was familiar with moments of nostalgic reminiscing where I would recall in a general way an experience from the past, the experience of suddenly being cast back on the *Camino* was quite different from these previous experiences. It was like split-second time-travel where I was actually transported to a specific instant on the trail. I was not remembering the experience - I was there. Another interesting thing about this time-travel was that I was never transported to the same time or place. One time I found myself on the street leading out of a small hamlet, another time I was walking the path by a river, another time I was enjoying the cool breeze at the top of a hillside. The thing that was noteworthy about these instances is that I had lived them with attentiveness and focus, free of the usual distractions that keep me from living the moment to the fullest. Adopting walking as our only means of transportation had made it possible for me to be present to life in a way that I had rarely been before. I had experienced the truth of Kosuke Koyama's observation: "Walking is the proper speed and the proper posture that can prepare man [sic] to meditate."[xxxviii]

In the same way, thanks to the shift in time and distance triggered by crisis, I experienced a renewed passion for life even before the actual diagnosis of breast cancer. I hugged my husband and my children with increased tenderness, I appreciated flowers with more delight, I sensed others' pain with greater empathy, I exercised with new-found vigor and purpose, and I prayed as if there was no tomorrow. I could now totally relate to David Power's explanation of

Path along flooded road in Galicia

why intervals of serious illness are times of such intense living:

> *Although it may appear a mere hiatus suspended in time, sickness is less halting-place than passage from a state of innocence, untroubled by intimations of mortality, to one of wisdom, able to perceive, through eyes opened by the confrontation of death as possibility, that human life must be lived within limit.*[xxxix]

Don Alonso was right. Both the pilgrimage to Santiago and the pilgrimage with breast cancer were special times. Through exposure to different rhythms of time and space, rhythms much slower and more focused than my usual frantic, scattered pace, I had discovered the mystery of life in the present moment. I realized that whatever the circumstances, whether trekking across northern Spain or trekking through a serious illness, all I had was the present moment. There is something incredibly awesome, frightening, and sacred about this truth.[xl] Thoreau expresses beautifully the breadth of sacredness contained in the present moment:

> *In eternity there is indeed something true and sublime. But all these ties and places and occasions are now and here. God himself culminates in the present moment, and will never be more divine in the lapse of all the ages.*[xli]

The re-assurance that God was fully present in all my moments of intense living, whether due to ecstasy or agony, encouraged me to contemplate the most challenging part of Don Alonso's second insight: *just as it was for Mary, once you have been "illuminated" or "called" by the Holy Spirit, the world will never be the same again*. With a great deal of trepidation, I read and re-read the words that I had carefully recorded in my daily pilgrim's journal: *once you have been "illuminated" or "called" by the Holy Spirit*. At first, the only understanding that I could glean from these words was the now all too familiar idea that God had chosen to send breast cancer my way. I continued to resist this understanding and squirmed under the weight of its implications. I had no problem accepting the idea that the world would never be the same again. I knew that my world would forever be changed by my experience with cancer.

The impasse in my understanding persisted until one day, when reviewing notes from the book *Mystical Passion: The Art of Christian Loving*, I came across McNamara's understanding of God's role and of our role in the scheme of life. "His [God's] own burning passion is *to let us be*; and our own human goal, our finest and final aspiration, is *to be*: fully, exuberantly, divinely." [xlii] I was ecstatic! Finally I had found an explanation of God's movement in the world, of God's movement in my life, that was life giving. The heaviness of confusion, anger, and guilt that I had harbored for weeks gave way to tears of relief and joy. I felt as liberated and free as I had those many times on the *Camino* when, at the end of a long, arduous day of walking, the backpack came off and there was rest.

McNamara's brief explanation not only affirmed the sacredness of each moment but, more importantly, it freed me to consider the Holy Spirit's call as invitational rather than coercive and punitive. I could now see that the call that Don Alonso was referring to was God's call to live life in the present moment. It was a call to be "conspicuously and contagiously alive,"[xliii] no matter what the circumstances. It was not a call to a specific circumstance such as wellness or illness, plenty or loss, pleasure or pain. Who was ultimately responsible for varying circumstances, I did not know. It was a question that the greatest scholars have not managed to explain with any degree of certainty. All I knew, all I could accept, is that God was inviting me to life. I could almost hear God saying to me, through Kabir's thoughtful poem:

> *Do you have a body? Don't sit on the porch!*
> *Go out and walk in the rain!*
> *If you are in love,*
> *then why are you asleep?*
> *Wake up, wake up!*
> *You have slept millions and millions of years.*
> *Why not wake up this morning?*[xliv]

Now that I knew that the *call* to this journey with breast cancer was God's invitation to life and not a test or a punishment, I turned my attention to preparing as carefully for this pilgrimage as I had for my pilgrimage to Santiago.

Chapter 3: Preparation
Intention – Fate

German pilgrims in the cloister of the Monasterio de Santa María la Real, Nájera

> ***Being ready mentally, spiritually, and physically makes us lighter on our feet, more adroit at making decisions, and perhaps can even help keep chaos at bay.***
>
> - Phil Cousineau, *The Art of Pilgrimage*[xlv]

Preparation

... each resource provided needed information

My mental preparation for the pilgrimage to Santiago began inadvertently while preparing for another journey. In October 1996, Bob and I were at the International Travel Clinic exploring our immunization needs for a short business trip to Venezuela. In order to determine which medications would be most appropriate the doctor asked us, in separate interviews, about other locations we planned to visit in the next few years. Still under the influence of Cowley"s Reader's Digest 'Camino' article, I enthusiastically explained my growing desire to do the pilgrimage to Santiago. The doctor smiled knowledgeably and shared that she had just finished reading *Pilgrim's Road: A Journey to Santiago de Compostela* by Bettina Selby. I jotted down the title of the book, excited about the prospect of delving further into my dream journey. Not surprisingly, not yet aware of my growing response to the call of the *Camino*, Bob had other exotic destinations in mind.

When I finished reading Selby's account of her pilgrimage from Vézelay to Santiago aboard her trusty bicycle named Robert, I was even more enthralled by this ancient pilgrimage route. I devoured another personal account, *El Camino: Walking to Santiago de Compostela* by Lee Hoinacki, and spent hours surfing the nascent internet for any additional scraps of information that might satisfy my growing, almost obsessive hunger to know more about this pilgrimage. My late-night forays into the amazing reaches of world-wide internet communication amused my three young adults and Bob. The kids thought it was hilarious to see Mom addicted to the internet while Bob threatened to call a popular radio psychotherapist with the question: "What shall I do? I've lost my wife to the net!"

Still, my internet searches were a critical part of my modern day response to what I now perceived as a call, and of my mental preparation for the journey. Although meager (in 1996) by today's standards, each resource provided needed information on some aspect of the *Camino*. The web site offered by the Confraternity of St. James (a London-based, non-denominational association of pilgrims founded in 1983 to promote the pilgrim routes to Santiago de Compostela) was one of the most useful in terms of practical information.[xlvi] It included current information on distances, geography, weather, accommodation, and contents of travel kits. In addition, the site introduced me to the Confraternity's extremely helpful guidebook, *The Camino Francés 1997*. Weighing only five ounces, this handy guidebook is updated yearly, using feedback from the previous year's pilgrims to make necessary amendments and corrections. It includes historical notes, descriptions of *refugios* (pilgrims' hostels), hours of operation, suggested donations, points of interest, descriptions of other accommodations including campsites, and exact distances between towns. It also includes a helpful array of local features ranging from directions to find vegetarian meals and English-speaking shopkeepers, to a warning regarding a guide who asks 2000 pesetas for a tour in English of Burgos Cathedral.[xlvii]

Authors Selby and Hoinacki further enhanced my mental preparation and resolve to do the pilgrimage to Santiago. The personal accounts of these two mature adults aged fifty and sixty-five respectively, convinced me that a forty-nine year old could embark on this arduous pilgrimage and expect to arrive at her destination a bit worn but still radiant with expectation and with an awesome sense of achievement. Through these accounts I also learned about the *credencial* or pilgrim record and about the *Compostela* certificate. The *credencial* is a document that is issued to *bona fide* pilgrims at the start of the pilgrimage. It presupposes that the bearer is making the pilgrimage for spiritual reasons. This is a distant successor to the *testimoniales* or testimonial letters issued by bishops to medieval pilgrims. These official authorizations entitled the pilgrim to certain privileges along the route and "enabled him [her] to escape being classified as an adventurer or pilgrimage profiteer."[xlviii]

In a similar way, today's *credenciales* or pilgrim records entitle pilgrims to certain privileges: access to *refugios* along the way and discounted *peregrino* meals. A *credencial* can be obtained from the cathedral authorities in Santiago or from pilgrim associations outside Spain. In my first communication with members of the Confraternity of St. James, I was delighted to discover that Canada boasted a fledgling pilgrim association formed in 1995 and known as The Little Company of Pilgrims Of The Way of St. James. It was good to know that when the time finally came to embark on this journey, I could order official *credenciales* from our own Canadian pilgrim association.

I also learned that, in addition to serving as proof of the pilgrim's sincere intent, the *credencial* also serves to mark progress along the route and to validate that pilgrims have completed the minimum distances necessary to earn a *Compostela*. Pilgrims on foot or horseback must complete at least the last one hundred kilometers of the route and cyclists must complete the last two hundred kilometers. Proof of pilgrim status and distance

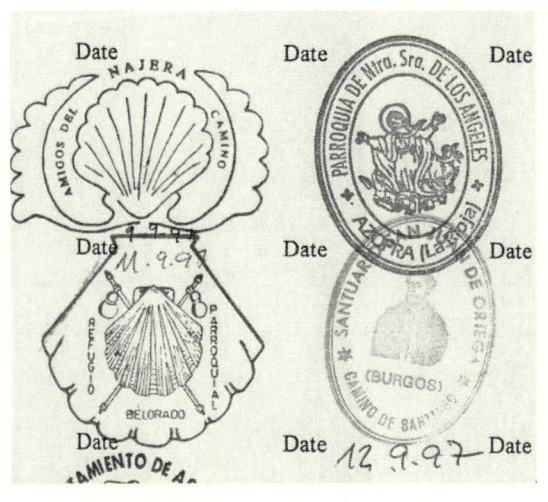

Sellos from Pilgrim's Passport

completion is achieved by having the *credencial* stamped each day at the *refugio*, church, bar, town office, or any other establishment that proudly carries a stamp (sello) of the town. At Santiago the *credencial* is presented at the pilgrim office near the Cathedral and a *Compostela* certificate is issued. This certificate is a copy of the traditional Latin document that originated in the fourteenth century. Through these many centuries it has served to officially designate those pilgrims who have completed the pilgrimage to Santiago. During the golden age of pilgrimage, eleventh to fourteenth centuries, the *Compostela* was the official proof that the sins of a deserving pilgrim were forgiven. Today, the *Compostela* is official proof that the pilgrim has gone the distance.

During the first quarter of 1997, I continued to read books and web site articles in a valiant attempt to satisfy my obsessive hunger for information on the ancient road to Santiago. Little did I know that, in less than two years, my now well-developed surfing and research skills would allow me to access information to satisfy yet another all-consuming hunger – the need to know more about DCIS so that I could more intelligently make the most important decisions of my life.

Preparation

... it was my breast, my body, my life, my future!

My mental preparation for the pilgrimage with breast cancer began the day I received the post biopsy results and lasted until the day of surgery – a period of roughly five weeks. This rather long waiting period was afforded me since my cancer was not invasive and I was diagnosed only a short while before the Christmas holiday season when medical teams and operating theatres are not functioning at full capacity. Although it is true that my journey began the moment I received the call from Dr. Lafrenière, I felt that the time leading up to the mastectomy itself was precious preparation time. This sometimes frustrating, sometimes enraging, sometimes enlightening period of five weeks allowed me to research my illness and to make the best decisions I could, based on its peculiarities and my needs.

During this assessment time, I became increasingly aware of how vital it was to my mental and emotional health to have a voice in the decisions that affected my life so profoundly. As I had on the *Camino*, I needed to take as much responsibility and ownership as I could for my new challenge. Through the diagnosis of breast cancer I had already experienced loss: loss of the future I had envisaged, loss of physical integrity, loss of naiveté, loss of much control over my own life. I did not want or need to add to these losses the loss of self-actualization and self-motivation that can easily become part of the sick person's role. In her article "Sickness and Symbol," Jennifer Glen describes the traditional role of the sick person with disturbing clarity: "It is a role of passive dependence in which the sick person relinquishes all autonomy, initiative and responsibility to those who play the complementary role of dispensers of care."[xlix]

When I shared Glen's description with my friend, Garrett, a professor of English, he pointed out that the words 'passive,' 'patient,' and 'passion,' are all derived from the same Latin root: *patior*, to suffer. I was shocked to discover that suffering had the potential of becoming an even greater part of my identity during this time. I could do nothing about my identity as patient: I had a disease that required medical intervention. And as for passion, thanks to McNamara, I now understood it as more than simply resigned suffering but rather as passionate engagement in life no matter what the circumstances. But suffering resulting from passive resignation I could resist and avoid. I desperately needed to feel that I was still, to some extent, master of my own fate. After all, it was my breast, my body, my life, my future!

I began my mental preparation as I had for the pilgrimage to Santiago – by accessing written sources for inspiration and for information. For my new pilgrimage, I relied heavily on *Dr. Susan Love's Breast Book* because it is such a complete resource on breast health and disease. Whenever I found a synoptic article on any aspect of DCIS, I would often cross-reference that information in Dr. Love's book. I found these hours of research emotionally and psychologically exhausting. I finally realized that through my exposure to so much information, I was immersing myself not only in my individual experience of DCIS but in the multiplicity of breast cancer possibilities documented in the literature I was reading. I was also submitting myself to the strong biases of individual authors and to the frightening array of anomalies that were not statistically representative of

Preparation

my reality. In spite of this realization, I continued to examine a wide range of resources with the intention of making well-informed decisions regarding treatment, possible reconstruction, and follow-up therapy. My need to search out more and more information was also fuelled by the hope that I would eventually find some definitive data with regards to causes, prevention, and cure for DCIS.

Although my research exacted an emotional toll, it enabled me to make preliminary decisions regarding treatment and reconstruction. The morning following the post-biopsy call from Dr. Lafrenière I accessed two web sites that clarified further my need and growing preference for a mastectomy. One of these articles was a review from the Annals of Internal Medicine dated 1 December 1997. Although I could not fully understand all the technical terms in the document I could work my way through the general themes and had no difficulty understanding the summary statements. In great detail, the contributors to this review reinforced what Dr. Lafrenière had told me the day before. Two statements were particularly pertinent to my situation: "The presence of *comedo necrosis* and surgical margin involvement are the most commonly used predictors of the likelihood of recurrence. . . . Mastectomy as primary treatment for DCIS is associated with near-total avoidance of recurrence."[l] Although the article also concluded that lumpectomy followed by radiation therapy was an appropriate treatment strategy for some types of DCIS, it was clear that for me the most prudent form of treatment continued to be a full mastectomy. I found the same hopeful conclusion in the second article: "For DCIS, total mastectomy . . . offers near-complete cure".[li]

As I began to understand more explicitly my particular need for a mastectomy, I became aware of a shift in my view of the impending surgery. Although I was still terrified and spent much time wondering what my life would be like after such a disfiguring procedure, I slowly started to see that this intervention, drastic as it was, was ultimately life-giving. Mentally preparing for the journey with breast cancer was not only providing me with the knowledge I needed to make the best treatment decision but it was also beginning to transform my view of mastectomy. I was beginning to see differently, to see with the "eyes of the heart," as the Muslim mystics, the Sufis, have long taught, and to "transform the inevitable ordeals of [my] journey into opportunities to learn something about [myself] and the wide world around [me]."[lii]

> *... I could have negotiated the trail without a breast ...*

Once I had concluded that a mastectomy was the most prudent treatment option for me, I turned my attention to the question of reconstruction. I never struggled with whether or not I would have reconstruction. This was a given from the moment I acknowledged the need for a mastectomy. The only question I debated was what method of reconstruction was best for me. I discovered that the plastic surgeon to whom I was referred offered two main methods of breast reconstruction. The most popular method involved forming a natural-looking breast using a flap of skin, muscle, and fat taken from another part of the body. Most often the flap of natural tissue is taken from the abdominal area. This procedure carries a slight risk of permanently weakening the abdominal muscles.

The second method of breast reconstruction involved the insertion of a saline implant. While this method is far less invasive than the first method, its results are not cosmetically as natural.

I opted for the saline implant reconstruction both because of its less invasive nature and, more importantly, because I did not want to risk compromising my abdominal strength. My pilgrimage to Santiago had awakened in me a powerful love of backpacking. Only six months before my diagnosis, Bob and I and two of our adult children had successfully completed Canada's West Coast Trail – a somewhat more secular pilgrimage. Stretching along 75 kilometers of one of the wildest coastlines in the world are coves, beaches, bays, rivers, waterfalls, rock ledges, caves and tidal pools, framed on the one side by the restless sea and on the other by the remnants of one of the Earth's most exhilarating temperate rainforests. Trail amenities include rough-hewn, slippery boardwalks, ladders (some with as many as 200 rungs), five cable cars, many bridges (some are slippery logs over deep ravines, some are suspension, some are regular), and washroom facilities humorously known as the "intertidal flush zone".

Climbing ladders with 12 kg pack
West Coast Trail 1998

Thinking back to this wilderness experience, I knew that I could have negotiated the trail without a breast or with an implant instead of a breast but I doubted that I could have completed such a rigorous trek with weakened abdominal muscles. I personally did not want to do anything that might hamper my ability to backpack. The ability to look forward to many more backpacking adventures provided brief respites from the isolation of my immediate situation and I did not want to jeopardize in any way those tenuous fragments of hope.

Not until my breast reconstruction was complete did I first become aware of the social and political issues surrounding reconstruction. The first murmurs came from my plastic surgeon during a follow-up visit. Dr. de Haas acknowledged that many of the women with whom he explores the possibility of reconstruction feel guilty for wanting this surgery. Not having experienced such feelings, I was shocked to think that some women were struggling with guilt in addition to the already excruciatingly heavy emotional burden sparked by this disease. I was even more horrified by the possibility that women who desperately wanted breast reconstruction, for whatever their individual reasons, might opt for no reconstruction in order to assuage their feelings of guilt. What gives rise to this guilt?

Dr. de Haas explained that one source of guilt is from well-meaning friends who have chosen not to have reconstruction. The knowledge that some women have moved forward to bravely face their new world one-breasted makes the newer initiate feel that if she does not do the same, she is less strong, less resilient, less adaptable, and definitely too vain. Another source of guilt for women considering breast reconstruction is the

Preparation

body of literature documenting other women's written accounts of their journeys. One of the most definitive accounts exploring the emotional and psychological reasons for not succumbing to any form of prosthesis or reconstructive surgery is, *The Cancer Journals* by the late Audre Lorde. These journals chronicle Lorde's journey with breast cancer, which began in the fall of 1978; her book appeared in 1980.

When I first picked up Lorde's book, I was shocked by her abhorrence of reconstructive surgery: "Within the framework of superficiality and pretence, the next logical step of a depersonalizing and woman-devaluating culture is the advent of the atrocity euphemistically called 'breast reconstruction'."[liii] These words reverberated so harshly through my consciousness that I was tempted to relegate *The Cancer Journals* to the return pile. Then I remembered the first statement in Lorde's introduction to her book: "Each woman responds to the crisis that breast cancer brings to her life out of a whole pattern, which is the design of who she is and how her life has been lived."[liv] I remembered these words of wisdom as I continued to explore the personal journeys of Lorde and other breast cancer initiates. Although this reminder helped me to accept that Lorde's account came from a place of deep integrity based on her own life experience, I still felt a strong need to reduce in some way the impact of her extremely powerful voice and to re-affirm my choice of reconstruction.

And thus I'll take my pilgrimage. I reminded myself that because my life experience was not her life experience and because there had been major improvements in breast reconstruction

67

techniques in the past twenty years, my view of breast reconstruction was hugely different from Lorde's understanding. Instead of seeing reconstructive surgery as an atrocity visited upon women by society, I viewed it as a gift, an advance in plastic surgery available to women that can help reduce in some small measure the traumatizing impact and social stigma of losing one or both breasts. Reconstructive surgery cannot eliminate the trauma of mastectomy; it can only make living with its aftermath more tolerable. I knew that, for me, reconstructive surgery was the right decision.

How different my language was from that of Audre Lorde! Although Lorde and I shared the common experience of breast cancer, our individual stories of that experience were unique and original. Our one-of-a kind stories would never be repeated. I now understood more fully the counsel of Anderson and Foley in their work on the power of the personal story: "Because we live in the stories we create, we need to be sure that the stories we live are shaped, in large measure, by our own vision of life."[iv] As I continued my mental, physical, and spiritual preparation for my ongoing pilgrimage with breast cancer, I resolved to remain true to my particular world view – true to the uniqueness of my own story.

Physical preparation for pilgrimage during the Middle Ages included paying one's debts, getting one's house in order, and outfitting oneself for the journey. The very real possibility that a mediaeval pilgrim might not return from the journey gave rise to strict ordinances concerning financial planning. The pilgrim was required to pay back any debts, make provision for his family during his absence and in the event of his possible demise,

Preparation

have enough money left over for the journey, and for the requisite alms giving. Pilgrims were also required to wear the appropriate pilgrim attire that identified them as *bona fide* pilgrims. This consisted of a long coarse gown with large sleeves, "a broad-brimmed hat, a scallop-shell badge indicating their passage, a satchel worn across the back called an *escarcela*, or scrip, and a *bordón* (a 'pilgrim's staff' or walking stick.") [lvi] Attached to the pilgrim's staff was a drinking gourd. In addition to being practical necessities for the journey these items were powerful symbols of the spiritual journey. Sir Walter Raleigh (1552–1618) expressed this symbolism in the following excerpt from the poem, "His Pilgrimage".

Statue of Santiago (wearing traditional pilgrim's garb) above the Puerta del Perdón, Catedral de Santiago

His Pilgrimage

GIVE me my scallop-shell of quiet,
My scrip of joy, immortal diet,
My bottle of salvation,
My gown of glory, hope's true gage;
And thus I'll take my pilgrimage.[lvii]

Today, physical preparation for an arduous walking pilgrimage includes many of the same issues that concerned mediaeval pilgrims: adequate financial resources for the traveller and for those left at home, and suitable clothing and equipment for the journey. In addition, modern pilgrims, most of whom live a rather sedentary lifestyle, need to give serious attention to adequate physical conditioning.

Part of our 'physical' preparation for our pilgrimage to Santiago included a visit to our lawyer to update our thirteen-year-old wills. Although the risk of death is very low for pilgrims today, we saw our five-week journey as suitable motivation to get our affairs in order. Our adult children were most relieved to be referred to as something other than the "infant children of" and Bob's sister and her husband were relieved that they were no longer named as guardians of the said "infant children of". Several times during this process I wondered at our lax approach to keeping such documents up to date. I concluded that the probable reason that we did not update our wills more frequently was that people do not often take time from their busy lives to think about and to plan for death, even though we cannot be surer of anything else in life.

Then came the crucial part of our physical preparation – conditioning our bodies! As already mentioned, prior to the experience of the *Camino* we had not been avid backpackers – we had merely been passionate day hikers. In preparation for the pilgrimage we added a new dimension to our weekend day hikes: brand new overnight backpacks weighted with kilos of sugar and flour. Except for these weekend excursions we did no other cardio or strength training prior to embarking on the *Camino*. Owing to the ordinary busyness of everyday life, we found it impossible to simulate

Preparation

a walk of twenty or more kilometers day after day. Thus we left to the *Camino* the ultimate conditioning of our bodies and minds.

The last part of our physical preparation for the *Camino* involved equipping ourselves with appropriate clothing and gear for the journey. A trip to one of the local outfitters provided us with: sturdy hiking boots in place of the mediaeval pilgrim's sandals, Gore-Tex jackets and pants replacing the coarse woven gown, and plastic water bottles substituting for the ubiquitous gourd. Taking to heart the advice "be prepared for the cool fall weather in the mountains" we procured down filled sleeping bags rated for -5°C (having failed to differentiate between fall weather in our 'southern' Canadian Rocky Mountains and the mountains of 'northern' Spain). Two indispensable items that resembled closely the accoutrements of mediaeval pilgrims were our hand-hewn walking sticks and our broad brimmed Tilley hats. With all of this and much more crammed into high tech backpacks we were ready for twenty-nine days of life on the *Camino*.

...my energies were all directed towards wellness and health ...

My physical preparation for the pilgrimage with breast cancer focused mainly on keeping my body as well conditioned as possible. Inspired by our new physical capacities achieved on the *Camino* and determined to maintain a high level of physical fitness, Bob and I had joined a fitness club shortly after our return from Spain. Although we were committed to this new endeavour, there were still weeks that elapsed where neither of us made it to the gym. My diagnosis of breast cancer instantly changed this hit-or-miss approach. I became a disciplined taskmaster and insisted that we work out every second day. I knew that working out or not working out could not change the diagnosis or the treatment plan. But I also knew that when I worked out I felt that I was taking at least some measure of responsibility for the condition of my body. I was reclaiming some degree of control and that was incredibly empowering. In sharp contrast to the antiseptic smells of illness and dread that tended to erode my personal sense of power and control, the pungent smells of physical strengthening and body toning were an invigorating reminder that I was more full of health than of ill health. Within the energetic surroundings of the gym, I knew I had the health I needed to train for this pilgrimage just as I had for the pilgrimage to Santiago.

And train I did. Particularly during the period of interminable waiting leading up to my mastectomy, I came to see my visits to the gym as a necessary lifeline. When I was at the gym my energies were all directed towards wellness and health – when I was away from the gym those same energies were free to dwell on the seriousness and the danger of my situation. Although I could not make the condition nor the journey go away, I could ensure that I was physically prepared for the demands of the journey. It was particularly important for me to work out at the gym on the nights prior to each surgery: biopsy, mastectomy, implant insertion. There was something akin to a ritual about this routine. Anderson and Foley claim that rituals "are essential media through which human beings create environments conducive to their psychological, social, and spiritual survival and development."[lviii] I believe that my need to workout just before surgery was my way of creating a life-giving environment that

... a change of heart as well as a change of pace.

Preparation

would support my survival on many levels. These workouts filled my consciousness with a sense of control, strength, wellness, hope; they released the recurring accumulations of toxic anxiety and fear; and they filled my body with the healing energy of cleansing oxygen. These night-before workouts also marked the movement from the preparation phase of the journey to another leg of the journey itself. I had prepared myself the best I could. Now it was time to step forward onto the path.

Spiritual preparation for pilgrimage during the Middle Ages was so important that failure to address spiritual concerns could invalidate the whole effort. In *Pilgrimage: An Image of Medieval Religion*, Jonathan Sumption writes: "A pilgrim who left without making amends to those he had wronged could not possibly make a sincere confession, and without a sincere confession, it was generally agreed that his pilgrimage would be worthless."[lix] For mediaeval pilgrims a pilgrimage was first and foremost a spiritual quest. Pilgrims sought a meaningful encounter with the holy and the forgiveness of their sins; they sought self-purification through the sacrifices and hardships of the road, and physical healing through contact with the relics of their favorite saints.

Mediaeval pilgrims who completed a recognized pilgrimage expected to receive the sought-after spiritual rewards. They expected a personal transformation. They expected to become "new creations" as promised by St. Paul in his second letter to the Corinthians: *"So from now on we regard no one from a worldly point of view. Though we once regarded Christ in this way, we do so no longer. Therefore, if anyone is in Christ, he is a new creation; the old has gone, the new has come"*

(2 Cor 5:16-17).

Modern pilgrims also set out expecting something significant to happen. To ensure that something does, they must also heed Paul's advice to move away from their usual worldly point of view. Pilgrims of today, like their counterparts of old, must break away from their habitual routines, roles, responsibilities, and cultural world views in order to see the world with imaginative, expectant eyes. As photographer and yoga instructor Trish O'Reilly explains: "If my trip is going to be sacred, I need to see differently. I need to think new thoughts, not just conditioned responses."[lx] Since a pilgrimage is a sacred journey with the express purpose of bringing renewed, expanded meaning to life, it requires a change of heart as well as a change of pace.

The very desire to embark on a lengthy, walking pilgrimage in our age of comfort and convenience demands the ability to see with imaginative, expectant eyes. This became very clear to Bob and me as we shared with friends and colleagues our dream of walking the *Camino* as a meaningful way of celebrating our twenty-fifth wedding anniversary. On these occasions the conversation came to an abrupt halt as those with whom we were conversing drifted as politely as possible to another side of the room. The cultural norm is that one celebrates this significant anniversary by basking in luxurious creature comforts at a resort location or by hosting a gala party for family and friends. The idea of celebrating such an occasion by walking twenty plus kilometres a day, wearing the same two sets of clothes day after day, and sleeping in single bunks night after night in the company of thirty or forty strangers was more than many casual observers could handle.

Without imaginative, expectant eyes it is impossible even to conceive of a world that is not defined by societal prescription. Spiritual preparation for the modern pilgrim involves choice, the choice of seeing the world through these new eyes rather than through resigned, myopic eyes. Cousineau explains that if our journeys are going to be sacred we must "move from a dependence on others' images of the world to *imagining* how [we] might walk [our] own path to the holy ground of [our] heart's desire."[lxi]

> *This catastrophic view of mastectomy...*

My spiritual preparation for my journey with breast cancer necessitated the determined use of imaginative, expectant eyes to counteract society's extremely negative view of mastectomy. Due to the pervasive fixation with women's breasts as public attributes of sexuality and beauty, society views the removal of a breast as a negative, debilitating, life-eroding experience for a woman rather than as curative and life giving. Even the removal of a diseased uterus, the receptacle of ongoing life and the ultimate organ of female sexuality, is not viewed with the same horror as the amputation of a breast. This catastrophic view of mastectomy is so ingrained in our society that a male friend of mine believes that this surgery is the worst thing that can happen to a woman. And the medical profession, inescapably influenced by societal norms, whenever possible presents lumpectomy followed by radiation as a less severe alternative to mastectomy – somehow minimizing the physical, psychological, and emotional impact of improved but still debilitating radiation therapy.

During the five weeks leading up to surgery, I struggled to overcome this horrifying societal view of mastectomy. I knew that it was critical to my psychological and emotional wellbeing that I develop my own unique understanding of this life-changing surgical intervention. Seven centuries ago, the Sufi mystic Mevlana Rumi had offered the following counsel: "Don't be satisfied with the stories that come before you: unfold your own myth."[lxii] I knew I had to unfold my own story, my own myth with respect to what a mastectomy would mean in my life. However, through some of the stories that came before me, I found a means of understanding and articulating my own story. One of these was the biblical story of Hezekiah.

The story of King Hezekiah's bout with a life-threatening illness and his subsequent recovery (Isaiah 38) chronicles God's healing power using the known medical practices of the day. The first six verses of this story read like the stereotypical miracle story. Hezekiah becomes ill to the point of death and receives a visit from the prophet Isaiah. Isaiah tells him to put his house in order since he is going to die. On hearing this, Hezekiah is overcome with grief and pleads with God to spare him. God hears his plea and sends Isaiah back to Hezekiah to tell him: "I have heard your prayer and seen your tears; I will add fifteen years to your life" (38:5). Verses ten to twenty then record Hezekiah's testimony of praise and thanksgiving in response to God's tender mercy. Up to this point, Hezekiah's recovery appears to involve an instant cure that does not require any recourse to medical intervention. It is not until the second last verse in the chapter that the reader discovers that Isaiah actually gives instructions for treating

Preparation

the malady using the medical procedures of the times: "Prepare a poultice of figs and apply it to the boil, and he will recover" (38:21).

Given my own life-threatening illness I resonated deeply with Hezekiah's story, with his grief, his terror, his pleas for mercy. And although I was relieved to see that God chose to heal him, I was even more thrilled to discover through verse twenty-one that this healing was not some sort of magical cure. Hezekiah's healing evolved in due process following the implementation of a known medical procedure. "Yes, God heals!" I thought. And She can heal, I was sure, in the beat of a moment, but does so more often through the medium of human procedures. My impending mastectomy was such a procedure. God's healing hand was poised to heal my body of the threat of invasive cancer by removing the diseased cells that had invaded my right breast. This surgical procedure, however frightening and disfiguring, was a gift of life from God, visible evidence that God continues to heal in our day as in the time of Hezekiah.

From the moment I accepted mastectomy as the necessary option for me, I sensed a need to develop some sort of ritual of thanksgiving and surrender leading up to the actual surgery. I had read the account of one woman who hosted a party of farewell the night before her mastectomy. As part of her surrender ritual she wrote positive affirmations to herself on yellow helium-filled balloons. She then released them and watched them float higher and higher in the night sky – a powerful reminder that with or without her breast she was a person of value, ability, and staying power. I had also read several graphically illustrated before-and-after photo essays that celebrated the beauty of the female body with two breasts, with one breast, and in the case of Stephanie Byram, without breasts.

I finally decided on a parting ritual that felt right for me. I chose to arrange a short photo and verse album that celebrated some of the greatest blessings of my life; I called this precious little book, *Réjeanne's Book of Blessings*. The first photos that I included were photos of my three children as new-borns accompanied by photos of each infant nursing at my right breast. Through these photos I celebrated my body's ability to give birth to three healthy babies and the health of my right breast in nurturing them through the first months of their growth and development.

"Réjeanne with her precious little ones"
from *Réjeanne's Book of Blessings*

Next I included photos, twenty some years later, of three fine young adults and of a husband, with whom I enjoy an enduring love affair. In addition to photographs, I included meaningful scriptural passages such as Isaiah 38, pictures of a few love offerings from concerned friends and family, and short inspirational verses. I ended the book with the words that John Wesley is reported to have repeated on his deathbed: "The best of all is, God is with us!" By the time the short, twenty-page book was complete, I felt that my life was so full of blessings that I could hardly contain my joyful gratitude.

Preparation

As I repeatedly thumbed through the pages of my little book of blessings and shared it with friends and family, I became aware of the dual roles of this powerful ritual. Through its creation this album brought some sense of meaning to my experience of breast cancer by placing the experience in the context of my life as a whole. This integration engendered in me a solid attitude of gratitude as I acknowledged the incredible blessings in my life. Sustained by this overwhelming sense of thanksgiving, I was better able to deal with my feelings of fear, grief, loss, and surrender.

Once completed, this precious little book provided a positive framework for talking about this experience with family and friends. My book of blessings expressed so clearly the goodness and vitality of life that it was impossible for me, or those around me, to wallow in negativity or pity. This little book took the horror out of my situation and rendered the experience of breast cancer less toxic. Anderson and Foley support this understanding of the dual role of rituals in our lives: "Rituals not only construct reality and make meaning; they help us fashion the world as a habitable and hospitable place."[lxiii]

...the Pilgrim's Blessing marked for me the true start of our pilgrimage.

An appropriate ritual of departure is the last significant element of spiritual preparation for pilgrims of any era. In the Middle Ages this ritual included attending a mass that celebrated the departing pilgrims, making one's confession, taking Holy Communion, and receiving the Pilgrim's Blessing. Once the ritual ceremony was over, pilgrims made their way to the road leading out of town. Oftentimes, friends and family members would join the departing pilgrims and walk the route for a short distance. As an additional way of boosting the pilgrims' courage and resolve, the whole entourage would sing Psalms or other hymns until it was time for those who were not setting out to return home, leaving the pilgrims to ponder more fully the enormity of their undertaking.

Most present-day pilgrims to Santiago consider the small Spanish hamlet of Roncesvalles at the foot of the Pyrénées to be the official place of departure. Ever since a hospital was founded here early in the twelfth century the monks of Roncesvalles have helped pilgrims. One of the services they continue to provide is an evening mass followed by a ritual blessing for departing pilgrims.

Scallop shell – still hanging on a backpack after completing Camino

On 30 August 1997, in Roncesvalles, Bob and I and our three young adults (who were able to join us for two weeks of the pilgrimage) attended Mass and participated in the Pilgrim's Blessing. Although we had already walked 26 kilometres to get to Roncesvalles, the Pilgrim's Blessing marked for me the true start of our pilgrimage. The text used for this blessing dates back to 1078 and includes a blessing of the pilgrims' emblems, scrip, and staff. One of the most significant emblems for pilgrims to Santiago is the scallop shell – the recognized symbol for St. James. In liturgical art, St. James is usually depicted as an elderly man with a book in his hand and scallop shells as adornments. Most pilgrims wear actual scallop shells on a cord around their necks or pinned to their hats or packs. Initially we opted for less obtrusive scallop-shaped pewter pendants bought at the well-stocked monastery souvenir shop. We carried them to the pilgrims' mass and, once they were duly blessed, tied them around our necks as a sign that we were now full-fledged *peregrinos*. (Before departing the next day, we relented and joined others in hanging "banging, bumping" scallop shells to our packs.)

On the evening we were commissioned, the Blessing of the Pilgrims portion of the rite was articulated in five languages: English, French, German, Spanish, and Italian. This ensured that each pilgrim present understood clearly the sacred significance of the pilgrimage he or she was undertaking. The words of the blessing reflect the mediaeval mindset that a pilgrimage is first and foremost an interior journey; a journey whose aim is to draw closer to the holy in hopes of gaining the ultimate celestial reward:

Blessing of the Pilgrims

Lord Jesus Christ, you taught us through the Apostle St. Paul that here below we have no lasting city and must always seek the heavenly city. Hear our prayers for these pilgrims we commission. May the Holy Spirit breathe his grace into their hearts; may he enliven their faith, strengthen their hope, and feed the flames of their love. May they thus make their pilgrimage in a true spirit of penance, sacrifice and expiation. May the same Spirit purify their minds from every evil thought; may he defend their hearts and give the constant help of his protection, so that they can reach the objective of their journey safely, and by means of this pilgrimage they are now starting merit to come one day to the heavenly Jerusalem. You who live and reign with the Father and the Holy Spirit, one God, forever and ever.[lxiv]

Following this moving ritual of departure, we reverently filed out of the thirteenth century Collegiate Church of the monastery, cognisant that we were treading on holy ground. We had just participated in a thousand-year old ritual – a ritual attended at this very location by millions of pilgrims over the centuries. They had stood in this church, prayed this blessing, walked on these stones and looked forward to the morning sun, much as we did – filled with a strange mixture of jubilation and trepidation.

Pilgrims with sore feet walk on the flagstones against the wall!

Preparation

This surgery would be a life-changing rite of passage.

The pilgrimage with breast cancer or with any other life-threatening illness is similarly replete with rituals of departure: administrative ritual, dress and diet ritual, and procedural ritual. Some of these rituals are intended for the comfort of the pilgrim but most are for the efficient administration of the process as a whole. There are no systemized spiritual rituals of departure unless (and until) the person in need of medical services takes control of her own process and becomes her own ritualist, usually with support and assistance from family and friends.

Even though my journey with breast cancer had begun two months earlier, I considered the day scheduled for my mastectomy, 13 January 1999, to be the true point of departure. This surgery would be a life-changing rite of passage. I knew that when I walked into that operating theatre I would leave behind not only a precious part of my physical being but also any remnants of invincibility and naiveté that I had been able to cling to during the preliminary parts of the journey. This was the day when the reality of cancer would be made manifest.

Although I had done some spiritual preparation in the preceding weeks, I knew I had to acknowledge this immense crossing-over point with a spiritual ritual of departure on the actual day of surgery. Like others about to embark on a hazardous pilgrimage, I needed a blessing to help me face the truth of my undertaking, to moderate my fear of the unknown, and to provide a reassuring, calming encounter with God.

To that end I asked Reverend Gordon Jackson, both friend and former pastor, to pray with Bob and me just prior to surgery. There was no thirteenth century chapel here, only a quiet corridor in the surgical wing. But no less sacred. No thousand year old liturgy but a personal, contemporary and somewhat extemporaneous blessing. And yet no less comforting for this one pilgrim and her husband. As Gordon's words faded and they called me forth to the surgical suite I knew that, with this blessing, I would be better prepared for what lay ahead.

Chapter 4: Journey
Passion – Resignation

Pilgrim passing marker near Melide – 79 km left to Santiago

As I walk this linear path I am aware of my own dying, finitude, mortality. My leaves are falling, seasons slip away, I am a pilgrim setting one foot before another on my own mortal journey. One foot before another, one step, another step, keep on walking, mindfully, gently, thankfully.

Brother Ramon SSF, *The Heart of Prayer*[lxv]

Yet each day I choose to walk;

When morning dawned on 31 August 1997, we climbed from our bunks and hastened to get ready for departure. Dressed in our modern pilgrim's garb – shorts, T-shirts, hiking boots and scallop shell pendants – we hoisted our nylon packs unto our backs and made our way to the road leading out of town. Unlike medieval pilgrims, we did not sing psalms or hymns to fortify our courage. For me, the reality of placing my boot-clad feet on this ancient road on the outskirts of Roncesvalles was encouragement enough. After months of reading and dreaming about this sacred pilgrimage I was finally at the crossroads between dream and reality. Waves of breathless ecstasy washed over my whole being. I was finally on the ancient road to Santiago.

The first day of our official walking pilgrimage was even more exhilarating than I had imagined. The sun shone brightly, holly bushes periodically lined the way, and the villages featured white stuccoed houses with brightly painted shutters and doors, each one topped with a red tile roof. After hiking six kilometers, we enjoyed a breakfast of bread, cheese, and hot chocolate at a bar in the village of Espinal. This was the first of many meals eaten in bars: in this region of Spain, as in many areas of Europe, bars also function as restaurants and coffee shops. Larger establishments sometimes have a separate dining room (*el comedor*) that is opened for the early afternoon and late evening meals.

Red Shuttered houses in Espinal

Journey

After leaving Espinal, we hiked another five kilometers to Viscarret where we stopped for rest, refreshments and lunch provisions. Then we were back on the trail for another ten kilometers of slogging under the hot midday sun. Luckily, the trail offered some stretches of shade within a forest of large spruce trees.

We diligently placed one foot in front of the other determined to reach the *refugio* at Zubiri before all the bunks were claimed, continuing to marvel at the frequent appearance of route markers that steadily pointed the way to Santiago.

Hand painted arrow plus modern tile marking the way

Since we had departed St. Jean Pied de Port three days prior, we had followed this dependable sequence of yellow arrows, yellow dashes, and yellow dots, all of which were hand-painted by members of local associations of *Amigos del Camino de Santiago*. These markers showed up on all types of surfaces: corners of houses, tree trunks, rocks, and fences, making maps virtually unnecessary. We even saw a yellow dot on a hay bale in the middle of a huge field. (The next day we would discover that even in cities as large as Pamplona we could find our way by being vigilant of the yellow arrows that appeared on buildings, on light standards, on curbs, and on downspouts.)

At less frequent intervals all along the *Camino*, official trail signs particular to each region backed up the hand-painted trail markers. The official signs usually included a scallop shell motif: sometimes yellow and stylized, sometimes cast directly into the concrete base of the marker. As we continued to follow the "yellow marked road", we were humbled by the conscientious commitment of today's human "markers of the way".

This day, already the third day of hiking since we stepped down from the train in St. Jean Pied de Port and started our climb over the Pyrénées, was also the day when the physical hardship and pain of a lengthy walking pilgrimage started to manifest themselves in earnest. In his journal entry for the day, our son David describes the pain, exhaustion, and dogged perseverance that were quickly becoming a way of life:

Approaching Zubiri
with sore feet and tired legs

I knew this would be hard but it is impossible to visualize or imagine the real struggle or pain unless you do it. So here we are, ten kilometers the first day, seventeen kilometers yesterday, and another twenty-one kilometers today. And tomorrow we will walk another twenty kilometers to Pamplona – one excruciating step after another. It is a struggle of will over whine. You know that you have to keep going and the slower you go, the longer it will take.[lxvi]

As we persevered along the ever-changing topography of the *Camino* during those first exhausting days, we came to understand first hand Martin Robinson's belief that a pilgrimage is a pilgrimage precisely because it contains pain and hardship:

> There is almost an expectation that a pilgrimage needs to contain a challenging physical ingredient in order for it to be a pilgrimage at all. It is as if the physicality of the experience is part of the defining experience of a pilgrimage. Without the hardship, a journey ... comes much closer to a holiday or outing. So, in a strange way, the pilgrim rejoices in the dangers, difficulties and hardships.[lxvii]

Although I do not remember rejoicing in the hardships of the pilgrimage, I do remember the sense of achievement at the end of each day. *"At the time it sucks, but it gives you a great sense of accomplishment when you finally arrive at your day's destination,"* wrote our daughter Danelle, seven days and one hundred and fifteen kilometers into the journey.[lxviii] Our daughter Nicole lists some of the physical ailments that often plague the walking pilgrim:

> *"We are all exhausted and very sore. I have huge sore spots on my lower back where my pack rubs continually as I walk, and I have blisters on the bottom of my big toes, but other than that, I just ache all over."*[lxix]

Surprisingly, the physical demands of the *Camino* did not cause any of us to even consider the possibility of abandoning our respective goals: the city of Logroño for Danelle, David, and Nicole, and the city of Santiago for Bob and me. Instead, the physical demands of the *Camino* served to strengthen our resolve to persevere, as our sense of accomplishment grew with the successful completion of each passing day.

In addition to providing a daily sense of accomplishment, the extreme physical demands of the pilgrimage served to accentuate a fundamental dichotomy, the incredible physical capabilities but also the intrinsic vulnerability and weakness of the human body.

As we repeated the daily regimen of walking an average of twenty kilometers carrying twelve to fifteen kilo packs, some of the bothersome ailments of the first week started to heal. Blisters were less frequent as our toes and heels established their rightful places in our boots, knee and back pain lessened as their respective muscles toughened to the new weight demands, and end of the day exhaustion was less severe as our bodies adjusted to our daily workout. We also started to notice an improvement in our cardiovascular capability and in our overall endurance and body tone. I was particularly thrilled with my newly developed level of physical fitness, since I was never particularly athletic and had never thought that at the age of forty-nine I would develop a love and a capability for backpacking.

At the same time as we were making daily gains in our physical fitness, we were also confronted with the reality that our bodies had certain limitations. We all continued to experience pain in our specific areas of weakness: David and Danelle continued to experience pain in their knee joints, Nicole and Bob persevered with nagging back pain and I often found my calf muscles tightening up in painful knots. In addition, we all

Journey

tolerated the pilgrim's nagging companion: foot pain. Although this pain was palpable for the duration of our respective pilgrimages, it was most noticeable for the first twenty or so steps of each stretch of walking and when we stopped. It is for this reason that, whenever possible, we sat as soon as we stopped and if we had to stand, we stood flamingo-style on one foot, giving the non-weight-bearing foot brief moments of pain-free respite. We were quickly learning that the physicality of the *Camino* was one of its greatest teachers and walking, one of its greatest gifts.

Walking I

> Blisters, sore knees, backache, fatigue,
> Yet each day I choose to walk;
> Step by energizing step, I move forward,
> What exhilaration, what invincibility!
> Step by sluggish step, I move forward,
> Oh the deterioration, oh the vulnerability!
> Step by hopeful step, I move forward
> Assenting to life …
> Assenting to death …[lxx]

Assenting to life

The day of my mastectomy was a mild winter day with no snow and a temperature near freezing. With surgery scheduled for two o'clock, I had lots of time to get ready. I packed a very small bag of personal essentials including my small album of blessings. I wanted it with me as a constant reminder that, with or without my breast, I lacked nothing. Once packed, I took a long, warm shower. As I gently lathered my right breast, I was overwhelmed with emotion. In a few short hours, my precious breast would be gone and my anatomy would be altered forever. A myriad of questions flooded through my mind. How painful would this surgery really be? Would my chest look gross? Would I be accepting of my new look? And what about Bob? How would he react to the new me? What would the pathologists discover once they examined the excised tissue? What if, in the five weeks between the biopsy and today, the cancerous cells had become invasive? There were so many frightening unknowns that all I wanted to do was get to the hospital and get this surgery over with.

When Bob and I arrived at the hospital we went through the necessary ritual of admission and then made our way to the elevator lobby. There we met Dr. Lafrenière who greeted us warmly and asked me, "Are you ready?" I responded rather tentatively, "As ready as I can be, I think?"

As we rode the elevator up to the surgery preparation unit, I kept wondering how ready I really was for the journey ahead. Those many hours of mental, physical, and spiritual preparation now seemed very distant. I felt vulnerable and terrified. I clutched the bag containing my precious little album. "Remember the blessings," I reminded myself, "Remember the blessings." Then my thoughts drifted back to the pilgrimage to Santiago and I remembered our preparation for that journey. Short of walking five hundred and fifty kilometers as preparation for walking five hundred and fifty kilometers, we could not have known ahead of time the extent of the physical demands of that journey. Similarly, regardless of how much preparation I had done, I could not know the fullness of the experience of mastectomy until I lived the

Journey

experience. The Spanish poet Antonio Machado captured this truth in two short lines:

> *Traveler, there is no path*
> *paths are made by walking.*[lxxi]

Walking towards Hunto

That far corner became our sacred space

When we reached our floor, I registered with the intake nurse and then Bob and I sat down to await further instructions. In a few minutes, friend and pastor Gordon joined us. I was so relieved to see him and so glad I had invited him to come and lead us through a ritual of departure. He suggested we move to the end of the corridor where there were a few chairs and considerably less activity. That far corner became our sacred space as we chatted and prayed together. We shared humour, read scripture, and asked God to see me safely through my surgery. The most important aspect of those few moments of quiet recollection was the intentional acknowledgement that God was in the midst of this experience. I received the ultimate reassurance that I craved – I was not alone. God was my inseparable companion. I would not walk this hazardous journey alone. In that assurance, I received the ultimate Pilgrim's Blessing and I was now ready to walk the road.

Roughly one hour later, outfitted in the "one size fits some" cotton hospital gown, I began my walk to the operating theatre. Bob was my faithful walking partner as he had been for the hundreds of kilometers of the *Camino*, except on this journey he would not be allowed to accompany me on the last few meters. Hand in hand we followed our guide through the labyrinth of corridors. Each step I took affirmed my decision to have a mastectomy. This was not a procedure that was being foisted on me. This was a life-saving intervention that I freely chose. Each step gave me an increased sense of control over my threatening situation. Each step supported my full awareness and participation in what was happening. Each step upheld my dignity, at least for a short while longer. "How different this journey would be," I mused, "if instead of walking, I was laid out on a gurney, my arm attached to an intravenous tube whose contents were busily robbing my consciousness of active participation." As the large doors of the pre-operative area flew open, I realized how lucky I was to be in a hospital that had made such helpful changes in hospital procedures.

Bob and I sat down to await further instructions – by now a familiar routine. The anaesthetist soon came over to verify certain bits of information and to check if I had any questions. His calm and professional manner was reassuring. Then Dr. Lafrenière and Dr. De Haas emerged through the swinging doors that led to the various operating theatres. I found their appearance rather comical and chuckled politely to myself: although I was aware that Dr. Lafrenière was an extremely tall man, I did not realize how tall until I saw him walking side by side with the much shorter Dr. De Haas. As they approached I was struck by the thought, "How wonderful! I have "Mutt and Jeff" as a surgical team!" [lxxii] To add to my suppressed giggles, Dr. De Haas was wearing bright yellow operating shoes that reminded me of Tweetie Bird. So here I sat only a few minutes away from major surgery sustained by Bob's loving presence and surrounded by delightful cartoon characters.

Again I was aware of how empowering it was to have these pre-surgery conversations while sitting in a chair. Free of sedation and able to converse from an upright position, I had a greater sense of equality and participation. Once all the questions had been answered it was time for the next leg of the journey, the walk to the operating theatre. It was strange to walk this distance without Bob. After a reassuring hug, I turned and followed the nurse through the huge swinging doors, down a short corridor, and into the assigned operating theatre. Then I climbed onto the operating table, my last conscious act of independence and consent.

Walking II

Fear, disfigurement, loss, pain,
Yet today I choose to walk;
Step by tentative step, I move forward,
What engagement, what empowerment!
Step by urgent step, I move forward,
Oh the helplessness, oh the vulnerability!
Step by hopeful step, I move forward
Assenting to life ...
Assenting to death ... [lxxiii]

... a pilgrimage is a shared journey.

Step by gruelling step, we pushed on towards Santiago in the company of pilgrims of all ages and from many different cultures. As we walked, talked, rested, and shared meals and dormitories, we became aware of a gentle transformation within ourselves and within our fellow pilgrims. The fervour of a common goal coupled with the demands and delights of the road were transforming a collection of independent strangers into a community of interdependent pilgrims. Within this nomadic community, the revered states of self-reliance and autonomy soon gave way to an acceptance of personal limitations and to a resulting openness to receive and to lend assistance. Laurie Dennett, former chairman of the Confraternity of St. James, believes that "... acceptance of dependence and inter-dependence is one of the *Camino*'s gifts to the walker..."[lxxiv]

Artist and veteran of the *Camino* Lupe Rodriguez explains the transformation this way:

> In such a short period of time you develop an intimacy which is rare in our daily lives. Perhaps this is due to the available time, or the plain fact that your body becomes the major topic of discussion. There is certainly no hesitation to share the gory details of punctured blisters, sore knees and twisted ankles. There are also magical moments when the repetitive soothing rhythm of the walk allows people to share openly...[lxxv]

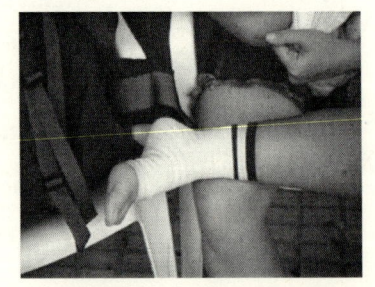

Another injured pilgrim ankle

Journey

Within our family and within the rich multicultural environment of the *Camino* each day brought opportunities to experience this gift of interdependence; of genuine reciprocity between individuals. On several occasions David carried some of his father's gear in order to ease the stress on Bob's back. One evening, our roll of duct tape made the rounds of the *refugio*. Consistent with its reputation, the duct tape served a wide array of uses - mending sandals, securing a loose pack strap, reinforcing a wobbly walking stick, and securing the on/off switch on a battery-operated toothbrush. On another evening, our muscle ointment was gratefully circulated among aching pilgrims, while a kind French woman applied first aid to one of Danelle's worst blisters. At the end of a +30 degree-day, a fellow pilgrim guided us to a private *refugio* that could only accommodate three more pilgrims. And almost every day, Bob helped fellow pilgrims to properly adjust their backpacks – a gesture that often brought instant relief of shoulder and back pain.

The reciprocal concern shared by fellow pilgrims was all the more amazing since encouragement, assistance, and explanations were often extended across linguistic barriers, as noted in the following journal entries:

> *I'm sitting here listening to a Spanish man and a German lady converse in English. He is assuring her, in his less than steady English, "I am certain you will get to Santiago." He hesitates frequently between words. I cannot hear her answer because her back is to me but I am aware of her lengthy pauses. "Things you will*

experience, you cannot expect," he adds. It is amazing to listen to them try so hard to converse.[lxxvi]

One of the Spanish fellows who we met last night discovered today that he cannot continue to walk the Camino. If I understood his gestures correctly, he has problems with his lungs. He thanked us for the use of the muscle ointment and then gave me his walking stick. He had bought the stick at the souvenir shop in Roncesvalles and it has the words, **Camino de Santiago**, *burned into the wood. This stick will always mean more to me than if I had bought it myself.*[lxxvii]

In addition to the growing inter-dependence among the community of pilgrims we were also becoming more aware of our inter-dependent relationship with the locals who lived along the pilgrimage route. We created commerce all along the route while the locals provided a wide array of much needed services. We found the *hospitaleros* (wardens) of the *refugios* especially helpful and encouraging. These people made sure that the *refugios* were open at the appointed time, registered our arrival, stamped our *credenciales*, and ensured that the doors were locked, usually at eleven each night. The commitment to the welfare of pilgrims exhibited by many of these volunteers is a testimony to the spirit of hospitality that has characterized the *Camino* since its inception.

In Najera, the kind warden allowed a young pilgrim who had developed gastrointestinal problems to remain in the *refugio* for several days at no cost. In Pamplona, an efficient warden arranged for medical aid for another ailing pilgrim. In Rabanal del Camino, the friendly wardens provided a simple breakfast of hot chocolate and toast for the departing pilgrims. And in Los Arcos one of the wardens made it his mission to act as cheerleader for all the pilgrims that passed through his *refugio*, as Nicole noted:

Only a few days left as we enter Galicia!

The refugio in Los Arcos was run by an older couple. They were very enthusiastic about their job. On the morning we left, the man was on the front steps sending everyone off with a hearty, "Buen Camino." When we approached the first town after hiking for five kilometers, we were surprised to meet the same gentleman, now walking back towards Los Arcos shouting encouraging words to all the peregrinos he passed. He must have had someone drive him to this town, so that he could then turn around and continue his role of cheerleader. I wonder if he does this every day he serves as hospitalero.[lxxviii]

This hospitalero was but one of several "characters of the *Camino*" we encountered; locals so fully committed to those passing by that they have become legendary among pilgrims. Madame Debril (as she did for years) sternly launched us on our way from St. Jean Pied de Port; Felisa welcomed us into Logroño with "figs, water & love";

99

Ignacio treated us and other passersby with family vinted Rioja Tinto wine; Anton surprised patrons at O Cebreiro with fresh-from-the-pot *pulpo* (steamed octopus). And, while we encountered neither the mythical refuge operator, Ramón, nor the much reported wild dogs of Foncebadón, many additional colorful characters filled-in to enliven our days.[lxxix]

The further we walked, the better we understood the truth that a pilgrimage is a shared journey. It includes the pilgrim, fellow travellers, *hospitaleros*, shopkeepers, trail builders, and a myriad of dedicated others – all of whom are committed to the pilgrim's safe travel and sure arrival.

All shall be well.

"Mrs. Taylor? Mrs. Taylor? It's time to wake up. Your surgery is over. You're now in recovery." As I fought to escape the dark grasp of the anaesthetic, a glimmer of consciousness sent panic and horror coursing through my veins. "No, this can't be," I thought. "This can't be me on a gurney! I could not possibly have had a mastectomy!" I desperately cried inside myself, from such a faraway place that no one could possibly hear me. "Mrs. Taylor, you're in recovery now. Your surgery is over. Would you like a sponge to moisten your mouth?" As the noise and the bright lights continued to hammer at my awakening consciousness, I was not at all sure that I wanted to return to the disfigured reality that I was slowly beginning to comprehend was mine. At one level, I wanted to wake up to the light and yet on another, I wanted to remain in the dark. Perhaps if I continued to sleep, this nightmare would pass and I would wake up free of any memory that it ever existed. Audre Lorde explains that "After a mastectomy, for many women . . . there is a feeling of wanting to go back, of not wanting to persevere through this experience to whatever enlightenment might be at the core of it."[lxxx] This was clearly my state of mind as I struggled to regain full consciousness.

And where was Bob? Was he not a part of this strange New World? Finally, after what seemed like a very long time (perhaps thirty minutes), he arrived and I was instantly transported into the Old World that I knew. As Bob bent down to kiss me, my fear subsided and I was overwhelmed by familiar emotions. I felt cherished, I felt loved, I felt safe. Surprisingly, my life seemed to be pretty much the same as before surgery – except for the residual confusion, the nausea, the sore throat, and the unbelievable thirst.

Bob quickly made himself useful by periodically handing me the refreshing, water-filled sponges, by holding my hand, and by gently stroking my cheek. At one point, he had to scoot to the foot of the bed so that the nurse could check my dressing. The flimsy cotton booties that I had worn on my walk to surgery were long gone so Bob lovingly started to rub one foot, and then the other, and then the first one again. How soothing and warm were his hands! How affirming! How calming!

As I yielded to Bob's comforting touch, my thoughts drifted from the recovery room to the *refugio* in Ribadiso de Baixo, a collection of several buildings beautifully situated beside a small, gentle river. Ribadiso was our second last *refugio* before arriving in Santiago. By this point we had spent twenty-seven days on the *Camino* and walked five hundred and twelve kilometers. Our day of travel to Ribadiso had been an arduous one, twenty-four kilometers and eleven rivers. We had walked down into eleven valleys and back up to eleven heights of land. One ascent was at least one kilometer long. After our lunch stop that day, I doubted that my calf muscles would loosen up enough to continue our walk to Santiago.

As we performed our end of the day activities at Ribadiso, my calf muscles progressively became tighter and tighter until every step became an agonizing effort. With two days of walking still ahead of us, we knew we had to do something to release the tightness in my calves. That night, after taking my customary place on the top bunk, Bob stood in the small space between the wall and the bunks and gently massaged Tiger Balm ointment all over my calves. Then he wrapped my towel around my legs and tucked them into my sleeping bag. As I lay there awake, for a few brief moments before dropping into a deep sleep, I felt the healing heat of the ointment penetrating deeply into my tight, over-stressed muscles. And I knew that the next day I would be able to walk the path again, if only "step by sluggish step".[lxxxi]

When my thoughts slowly drifted back to the recovery room, to Bob's touch, and to his unconditional love, I knew that I would be able to continue this frightening journey. As in Ribadiso, I had the loving support of my husband. As in Ribadiso, I felt God's healing touch permeating through my whole body. As in Ribadiso, I was reminded of the human body's amazing ability to rally after excessive physical exertion or trauma.

Journey

And, as on the Camino, this journey with illness was a shared journey. It included myself, Bob, our children, family and friends, a host of medical professionals including researchers, the hospital kitchen and maintenance staff - all of whom were committed to my well-being and to my full recovery.

With a good night's rest, I knew that tomorrow I would be able to move on. As I drifted in and out of drug-induced sleep while still in the recovery room, I experienced the reassurance expressed so beautifully by Julian of Norwich: "All shall be well, and all manner of things shall be well."[lxxxii]

There's no discouragement Shall make him once relent

On this, our second last day on the *Camino*, Bob and I rose early, had a quick breakfast, hoisted our packs onto our backs, and left Ribadiso in the moist stillness of early morning fog. Such fog is very common in Galicia, a region that is proudly known as *Galicia verde* (green Galicia). We proceeded along twenty-three kilometres of fairly smooth paths, weaving through a pleasant eucalyptus forest and past or through towns that were starting to have a more urban feel to them. By mid-afternoon we were

Pilgrims departing in early morning fog

registering at Arca's relatively new *refugio* along with many of our fellow pilgrims. This would be our last stop on the *Camino* – only eighteen kilometers left to Santiago.

Since the few bars in Arca did not offer meals, we all made good use of the spacious well-equipped kitchen to prepare sumptuous farewell dinners. Bob and I, as had become our custom over the past week, shared a meal with Ana, Jorge, and Sandra. Ana and Jorge hailed from Madrid: Sandra from São Paulo, Brazil. We had met this trio ten days earlier at the *refugio* in Rabanal del Camino and since then they had become as family. Ana and Jorge were good friends who had

Sharing journals and coffee after a final Camino meal.

started the pilgrimage together in the city of León, met up with Sandra in Astorga and quickly welcomed her as a third travelling partner. In explaining this generous gesture, Ana simply shrugged her shoulders and said: "It is simply a response to the spirit of the *Camino*. On the *Camino* people behave differently, they are more friendly and more open to receiving others into their midst."

As we gazed around the community dining room that night, we noticed that there were bottles of *vino* at virtually every table. There was an atmosphere of cheerful celebration as friends from all over the world once again shared their stories of hardship, of achievement, of discouragement, of generosity, of angels in disguise, of awesome wonder at the profound mystery of the *Camino,* and of regret that this utterly transforming experience was quickly drawing to an end.

At our table, Ana expressed heartfelt regret that the journey was almost over. I found this sentiment somewhat surprising since Ana had suffered more than most on this ancient road. She had experienced severe knee pain throughout the journey. Her discomfort was at times so severe that she had to hitchhike to relieve the stress on her knees. When she did walk, she could only walk very, very slowly. In order to keep up with Jorge and Sandra, Ana would often leave the *refugio* two hours before her travel mates. It was the only way that she could complete the suggested distance for the day. In spite of the constant pain, she persevered and each morning she was prepared to set out again. Ana's resilient determination to continue the journey epitomized for the rest of us the steadfast perseverance that marks the true pilgrim. This perseverance is aptly described by John Bunyan in his classic 1678 work, *The Pilgrim's Progress*:

> Who would true valour see,
>   Let him come hither;
> One here will constant be,
>   Come wind, come weather;
> There's no discouragement
> Shall make him once relent
> His first avow'd intent
>   To be a pilgrim.[lxxxiii]

Later I would reflect on the emotions Ana expressed as the end of our journey neared. Our lives had taken on a new and familiar routine: strapping on boots and backpack, walking all day, hand-washing clothes, eating. and falling into bed exhausted. But aware that, once we reached Santiago, our lives were about to undertake another significant shift. The normal lives we would return to, the familiar old friends, the old patterns would no longer be "normal" for the pilgrimage had changed us in a fundamental way. Aware that everything we needed to get by had been carried in our backpacks for four weeks (and some of that was deemed excess) caused me to wonder if the material things that we valued in our lives would still be as important. And so, like Ana, we too faced the last day of walking with a mix of emotions – excitement that we were within five hours walk of the Cathedral; disappointment that we would be saying goodbye to new-made friends; anxiety about our return and re-entry to our 'old' lives back home.

In years to come, I would discover a similar set of emotions as the formal part of various treatments neared their end. During months of a pilgrimage consisting of cycles of imaging, bloodwork, treatments, and surgery my life had a certain Camino-like routine. I had made new friends during each of these phases and, then, as I approached the end of treatment I experienced a similar anxiety. Again, my life and my body had undertaken a significant and permanent change. Again, I would be parting with new-made friends. Again, I had anxiety about returning – not to my 'old life', but to a new and uncertain future – one that would be filled with both promise and fear. [lxxxiv]

Over another glass of *vino tinto*, the five of us pondered further the role of pain and suffering in our experience of the *Camino*. Would our approach to Santiago have held the same exhilaration and sense of accomplishment had we not suffered along the way? Was not the experience of pain, exhaustion, and discouragement part of the fabric of this memorable experience? Through the struggle and intimate sharing we had experienced life in all its mystery and misery, its challenge and abundance. We had explored our limits and in so doing learned to rely and to help one another. Father Stephen Canny affirms the valuable role of suffering in our lives: "You are more alive after you have overcome something difficult. You're changed by the mountain and the fact that you have confirmed your faith. It's a remarkably effective way to answer the question: What is my purpose?"[lxxxv]

...tears flowed unashamedly

The night hours following surgery were anything but restful. Shortly after Bob left my bedside at about 10:30 PM a vicious migraine seized control first of my head, then of my mind, then of my body, and finally of my soul. As I lay there in excruciating pain, I could no longer think, I could no longer hope. All I wanted was for the pain to go away. I called for help but was told that nothing could be done. Ingesting any anti-inflammatory drug could seriously hamper the healing process by constricting the blood vessels around the incision area. I was left alone in the painful darkness, feeling betrayed by my body, feeling abandoned by those who were here to care for me. I cried out to God, to my departed mother to please help me. But no help came. The pain raged on. I felt as destitute and alone as I have ever felt in my life.

The tears flowed unashamedly for much of the night. Although my tears flowed out of intense physical pain, I soon realized that they were also pouring out a backlog of emotional pain. I had lost my right breast a few hours earlier. I would forever be disfigured. I was now a *bona fide* cancer patient. I was frightened of what the pathology work might reveal. I was terrified of what lay ahead. And so I spent my first night after surgery – desperately alone in the open, frank company of the darkness and of my tears.

In the ensuing hours, the assurance I had experienced while still in the recovery room completely evaporated. Through the clamour of the tenacious migraine, I was keenly aware of my natural limitations and weakness in the face of this continuing health challenge. I was also faintly aware that since my diagnosis I had enjoyed a surprising closeness, a kind of emotional and spiritual intimacy, with God, with Bob, with family, with friends.

I was beginning to realize that, just as the rigors of the *Camino* broke down the barriers of self-sufficiency to allow pilgrims to be there for one another, the demands of this journey with cancer had shattered the bold front that I usually presented to the world and made it possible for me to ask for and to accept the support, help, and prayers of family and friends. "Weakness helps us remember that our very lives are in God's hands ... The acceptance of natural limits seems to be a corollary to wholehearted receptivity to the unlimited bounty of God," [lxxxvi] and to the unlimited generosity and love of others.

Chapter 5: Arrival & Return
Compassion – Self-Interest

Catedral de Santiago de Comostela

For pilgrims of centuries past, the sight of the towers of the great Cathedral of Santiago from Monte del Gozo (Mount of Joy) signalled that arrival was assured. The shrine was only another five kilometers away. From this hilltop these earlier pilgrims could finally see the object of their prolonged hardship and suffering – the shrine of their beloved St. James. For them, arrival at Santiago was in some ways more significant for the next life than for this one. From his vantage point atop Mount of Joy in 1495, a Servite monk named Hermann Künig von Vach expresses his hope in the heavenly rewards to come:

> *From a mountain top, at the foot of a cross stuck in a mound of stones, pilgrims marvel at how beautiful the city is. May the pure Virgin Mary and her beloved Son help us devotedly reach St. James so that, in the life to come, we may find our reward and receive the celestial crown that God has granted St. James and all the Saints in the Heavenly Court.*[lxxxvii]

For Bob and me, setting foot in the great Cathedral of Santiago signalled our arrival. We entered by the side door shortly after 8:00 PM on the 26 September 1997, twenty-nine days and five hundred and fifty-three kilometers after leaving St. Jean Pied de Port. At this hour the Cathedral was respectfully quiet, with only a few stragglers like ourselves

Réjeanne placing hand on Jesse Tree at Santiago Cathedral entrance

seeking solitude and rest at the end of the day. We fulfilled a few of the customary rituals of arrival: placing our fingers in the well-worn grooves of the Jesse tree,[lxxxviii] hugging the bejewelled, larger-than-life statue of St. James, and walking past the reliquary that is said to house the Saint's remains. Then we sat down to pray in the age-old silence of this holy sanctuary.

No sooner had we settled ourselves in the pew than we heard the rain starting to fall in earnest on the roof of the cathedral. This was the first downpour we had experienced during our entire four weeks on the *Camino*. In hushed amazement we began to recite: "The rain falls lightly on Santiago" – the first line of the poem our son David had written **in advance** of our pilgrimage and which was printed on the inside front cover of our pilgrim journals.

Renewing

> The rain falls lightly on Santiago
> Holy on one thousand year cyclic duff
> Echoing the learning of each new step
> A modern pilgrim, rethinking drama,
> Reassessing foundations, hoping, I
> Trudge behind, meeting Jesus as a man.[lxxxix]

As we recalled the rest of David's poem we realized that in six brief lines he had captured (and foreshadowed) the essence of our pilgrimage experience and that he had named the subject of our longing – the person of Jesus.

That next day after the operation was an incredible high Dr. Lafrenière was the first person to check in on me the morning following surgery. Still under the stupor of morphine and of the abating migraine, I faintly heard him explain that he had found the DCIS to be very extensive and that my decision to have a mastectomy had clearly been the only choice. I registered his words and his accompanying concern as a matter of simple fact, subconsciously refusing to consider their sobering implications.

By lunchtime the morphine was discontinued, the post-anaesthesia stomach upset had subsided, and I had already received encouraging visits from my brother, from my beautiful daughters, and from Gordon. As Bob and I settled in to spend the quiet afternoon hours together, I was increasingly aware of a growing sense of euphoria. This is a common response to the day after surgery. I could identify fully with Lorde's description of her post-mastectomy high:

> *That next day after the operation was an incredible high. . . . The pain was minimal. I was alive. The sun was shining. I remember feeling a little simple but rather relieved it was all over . . . . I stuck a flower in my hair and thought "This is not as bad as I was afraid of."*[xc]

In addition to my feelings of euphoria, I had a keen sense of accomplishment since I had completed several of the most difficult and frightening legs of the journey: the five-week wait to surgery, the surgery itself, the recovery room awakening, the first night migraine, and the post-anaesthesia nausea. "I've come a long way", I concluded.

I reflected on these milestones as I had on the completion of each day's distance on the Camino. Only this time I did not receive a cello (stamp) in my pilgrim's passport (credential). Instead, my recovery was marked by the completion of each slow walk along the corridors, Bob on one side and my intravenous pole on the other, mentally recording and reinforcing my strong sense of arrival and achievement.[xci]

> *I now had to face the next steps of the journey and move on.*

Much as my arrival in Santiago had been followed by a pilgrim's letdown, my post-surgery high soon gave way to feelings of disappointment, uneasiness, and fear as I realized that I could not remain in the euphoria of arrival. I now had to face the next steps of the journey and move on. For pilgrims in the Middle Ages, moving on meant retracing their steps all the way back home – through the same hazardous, life-threatening territory. At least I was spared that challenge, unless at some point my remaining breast also became diseased. For the time being, moving on meant moving forward to as yet unexplored sections of the journey.

When Dr. Lafrenière came to see me on my second morning in hospital, I was able to explore with him the significance of his observations at the time of surgery. He explained that with the extent of DCIS present, there was always the possibility of micro-invasion. If the pathology work indicated micro-invasion, there would be a need for subsequent surgery to investigate the lymph nodes. Those results would then determine whether or not additional forms of treatment would be required.

I was overwhelmed by disbelief and panic. When would this nightmare end? It seemed like every result just led to more questions, to more concerns, to more challenges. It seemed like no matter how many difficult hills I climbed, there was always one more waiting for me around the next bend. "God, why don't you make it stop!" I cried.

Sometime later, as I reflected on the suffering inherent in a journey with a life-threatening illness, I remembered Bob's journal entry the night we sat listening to the rain in the great Cathedral of Santiago:

> *How true it is that we meet Jesus along the trail or in the wild places, or in the bars and refugios of the Camino. It strikes me how through all the gold leaf, all the carved figures, all the columns and archways and windows, we have tried to build some sort of Holy palace to capture some of God here with us. How badly we seem to have missed the point. God in Jesus has already willingly come to be with us here on earth but not as a crowned king in royal robes and*

Cruz de Ferro

Arrival and Return

palatial settings. He [Jesus] found His place along the trails and in the bars and restaurants of His own Camino.[xcii]

"And," I thought, "He also found His place of suffering along His *Camino*, as I had mine." I had not been alone and God had been more than my inseparable companion. God was and continues to be my co-sufferer. God suffers with me: intimately, fully, unreservedly.

Chapter 6: Blessings
Wholeness – Infirmity

L'Amour by Armand Coté, Private Collection

And I pray that you, being rooted and established in love, may have power, together with all the saints, to grasp how wide and long and high and deep is the love of [God], and to know this love that surpasses knowledge – that you may be filled to the measure of all the fullness of God.

Ephesians 3: 17-19

The morning after our arrival in Santiago we returned to the Cathedral to participate in one more ritual of arrival, the *Misa de Peregrinos*. Much as the Mass and Pilgrim's Blessing in Roncesvalles had marked the official start of our pilgrimage, the Pilgrim's Mass in the great Cathedral of Santiago designated the official end of the tangible part of this journey. To our amazement, the Cathedral, which only the night before had echoed with the tranquil sounds of the Holy, now reverberated with the brash presence of busloads of tourist "pilgrims". The activity of so many people milling around, pointing, chatting, and snapping flash photos made it extremely difficult to experience the sense of sacred space that we had experienced in the empty cathedral the night before. Then, we had been very mindful of God's words spoken to Moses in Exodus 3:5: "Take off your sandals, for the place where you are standing is holy ground."

Despite the now frenzied atmosphere of the Cathedral, the liturgy of the Mass managed to foster an atmosphere of meaningful community worship. At one point in the service, four recently arrived *peregrinos* were invited to share a prayer of thanksgiving for their experience of the pilgrimage and for their safe arrival. We heard these prayers in Spanish, German, English, and French. I found the words of the French pilgrim particularly moving:

> Thank you God for the opportunity to travel through your beautiful creation: the breathtaking Spanish countryside, the quaint villages, the lush and fertile fields, the ripe vineyards, the yards full of roses. Thank you for our fellow pilgrims and for the

generous folks who we met along the way. Help us to continue to live and to share the spirit of thanksgiving and generosity that we experienced on the Camino.[xciii]

These words captured the essence of the sixth phase of pilgrimage, the need to integrate and to share the blessings garnered along the way.

I heard these moving words two and one half years ago. Between then and now I have walked several phases of my second pilgrimage. Both journeys have overflowed with suffering, choice, and blessings – surprise blessings from the most unexpected sources, blessings of community (past and present), and blessings of intimate couple love. Sharing several of these blessings is my way of giving thanks and serves as a reminder of "how wide and long and high and deep is the love of [God]". (Ephesians 3:18)

29 Sept '97 Pilgrimage completed we made our way to the Santiago train station and positioned ourselves in the Customer Service queue. Once our turn came we discovered that the attendant spoke neither French nor English and had apparently earned her position through seniority rather than a real sense of customer service. As we struggled in our minimal Spanish to purchase tickets out of Santiago, from nowhere appeared a French-speaking Spanish businessman who interceded on our behalf. Without his "surprise" intervention, who knows where our tickets would have taken us?

6 Apr '99   This morning the Funky Winkerbean cartoon strip filled me with a joyous, exhilarating sense of well-being that remained with me all day. It reminded me again of the healing power of the selfless, unconditional love of a lifetime partner.

Lisa's Story printed 06 April 1999

This touching interchange between Les and Lisa takes place about a week after her mastectomy.

Created by Tom Batiuk, this series is entitled "Lisa's Breast Cancer Story" [xciv] and chronicles Lisa's journey with breast cancer from suspicion, to diagnosis, to biopsy, to mastectomy, to chemotherapy, to ongoing life. Serendipitously, this series started in one of our local newspapers only five days after my mastectomy. During my period of physical convalescence, this cartoon series became a significant source of emotional and psychological healing. As I eagerly followed Lisa's story, I felt less alienated and isolated. I could identify with every step of the process, with every emotion, with every interchange between her and Les, and with her desperate struggle to maintain some sense of normalcy. Through Lisa's story, I came to appreciate that my story was not simply an isolated anomaly, and that God heals through humour and the creative work of cartoonists.

18 Sept '97

Marie-Françoise, the Belgian mid-wife we had met only two days ago in Rabanal del Camino, was at the door to greet us when we arrived at the Villafranca *refugio* at 8 PM. We had trekked thirty kilometers that day in temperatures exceeding 30° C. We were hot, sweaty, sore, and exhausted. Without hesitation Marie-Françoise, who had already showered and changed into clean clothes, gave our sweat-soaked bodies a huge bear hug and kisses on both cheeks. We were overwhelmed by her spontaneous, unconditional gesture of affection. An angel surely had welcomed us home for the night!

4 Sept '97

Attended *la misa* at the Church of Santa María in Los Arcos. The rosary recited in Spanish preceded the Mass. Although the words were foreign to me, I was very aware that I was participating in a tradition that is very much a part of my spiritual heritage. The Mass was attended primarily by white-haired matrons – I saw my late *maman* in each one of them. Although she would not have understood the language any more than I did, *maman* would have been very much at home here and would have connected in a meaningful way with her Spanish-Catholic sisters. Throughout the remainder of the Mass, I became more and more aware that *maman,* grandmother *Joséphine,* and

Iglesia de Santa Maria, Los Arcos

great grandmother *Philomène* were as near to me as the living, perhaps even nearer. I was experiencing the great mystery of the community of saints, a community aptly described in *The Pilgrim's Progress*:

> There we shall be with seraphims and cherubims, creatures that will dazzle your eyes to look on them. There also you shall meet with thousands and ten thousands that have gone before us to that place; none of them are hurtful, but loving and holy; every one walking in the sight of God, and standing in His presence with acceptance for ever.[xcv]

14 Sept '97 The Cathedral of León is incredibly beautiful – the stained glass windows (over 100 of them) apparently rival Chartres Cathedral in France. The grandeur of the interior – ceiling height of 80 to 90 feet – takes your breadth away as soon as you walk through the Santa María la Blanca portal. I was just in time for the rosary which preceded Sunday Mass. The cathedral was filled with worshippers and tourists. I am now responding out loud when the rosary is said. I respond in French while those around me respond in Spanish. The identical rhythm is mysterious, musical, and holy. We truly are one community of believers across the miles.

Following communion, I once again had a powerful sense of *maman's* presence. I would have given anything for her to actually have been there in body so that we could have shared a hug. In some ways, she was very much present and we did share a loving embrace.

15 Jan '99 Two days after my mastectomy I was alone in my hospital room desperately wishing that my mom was still alive and with me. Then I remembered how frail she was just before she died. Now, four years later, she would have been even frailer. "No," I thought, "my dear mother would not need the worry of a daughter with breast cancer. It was best that she be with me from the place of seraphims and cherubims."

17 Sept '97 After leaving the private *refugio* of Tomás in the semi-abandoned village of Manjarin, the sky cleared again and we enjoyed beautiful views of the valleys below. Good day to walk as it was cool with regular cloud cover. At one point on the shoulder of the highway, Bob stopped walking and turned around to wait for me. Our eyes were full of tender love and anticipation. As I walked the several meters to meet him, we both knew that we were soon to share a most tender kiss. What a holy moment! It reminded me of slow-motion segments of movies where the woman runs to the waiting arms of her lover, long hair and flowing skirt billowing in the wind. We are neither glamorous nor famous (glamour does not exist on the *Camino*) but we do share God's awesome gift of love.

18 Mar '00 Today I reflected again on the familiar Biblical passage that describes Jesus' action of washing his disciples' feet on the night before he died:

> . . . *so he got up from the meal, took off his outer clothing, and wrapped a towel around his waist. After that, he poured water into a basin and began to wash his disciples'*

feet, drying them with the towel that was wrapped around him (John 13: 4-5).

The description of this intensely sensuous gesture reminded me of Bob's similar gestures in the *refugio* in Ribadiso when he had rubbed ointment on my calves and in the recovery room when he had massaged my feet. Sensitized by these experiences, I recognized for the first time the deeply intimate nature of Jesus' action. Not only was God my constant companion and my co-sufferer but now I knew that the God in whom I believed was also a God of intimacy – a God who desired to be in meaningful relationship with me.

20 Jan '99 "For this reason a man will leave his father and mother and be united to his wife, and the two will become one flesh" (Ephesians 5: 31). Although I have long known this passage with my intellect, today I came to know it completely and passionately with every cell of my being. For the first time since the mastectomy, Bob and I were drawn to share sexual intimacy. The moment we acknowledged our desire, I was overwhelmed by a strange mix of emotions. I was self-conscious and frightened. I saw with exaggerated clarity the aftermath of the surgery: a small mound where my breast had been, a four-inch incision still covered by a steri-strip, and the conspicuous absence of my nipple. Although Bob had already seen all this and affirmed my attractiveness several times, I still wondered if in the act of lovemaking my altered anatomy might prove to be repulsive to him. I decided not to risk this possibility and I adroitly kept my shirt draped over my right shoulder. As soon as Bob noticed what I was doing, he gently moved the shirt away from my wound and said: "Réjeanne, there's no need to cover up. It's part of us now."

I was overwhelmed with awe, with relief, with joy, with love for this man with whom I shared every aspect of my life. "It's part of us now" – five little words that brought more healing than I could have imagined. "It's part of us now" – five little words that announced clearly that we had truly become "one" as the apostle Paul had promised in his communication to the Ephesians. My wound was Bob's wound. Again, I was reminded of the image of God as co-sufferer.

14 Mar '99 This morning as I sat in church, my thoughts drifted back to the many sacred places we had visited during our pilgrimage in Spain, and to a graduate course, "Sacred Places; Sacred Spaces", that I had completed just days before departure. Much of my work focused on the distinction between sacred spaces of the natural world – mountains, rivers, canyons, plateaux, and rock formations – and sacred spaces that are the result of the creativity of men and women – cathedrals, temples, stone mounds, and medicine wheels. For the first grouping I had retained the name "sacred spaces". The second

Flagstone bridge near Melide

category I identified as "inspired spaces", the main differentiating feature being the application of human creative energy.

As I sat in church, musing over this distinction, new applications for the terms "sacred" and "inspired" crept into my mind: grapes and wine, grain and bread, stones and sculptures; yes, even breasts and reconstructions. It had become apparent to me over the last two months that I could no longer refer to my original breast and my reconstructed breast collectively. I no longer had a pair of breasts, I had one breast that was natural and that had been part of me for many years and I had another breast that was a brand new creation.

Sitting in an inspired space, I had found the language I needed to define the source and the uniqueness of my dissimilar breasts. My remaining, original breast was sacred. It was part of my evolution into this world, part of my femaleness, part of my ability to nurture and to love. My new breast, which I was learning to appreciate and to love, was inspired. Plastic surgeons, inspired by the sacred archetype of breast, use their creative energy and skill to fashion inspired breasts that can ease the pain of loss and restore some sense of symmetry and balance to the female form. I was amazed to discover that two small adjectives could bring such helpful clarification and additional meaning to my experience of mastectomy. Thank you, God, for the healing power of language!

Like the yellow marks that dependably pointed the way to Santiago, the stories of blessing that I have shared all point the way to a God of love. The experience of pilgrimage, whether to a holy site or with a life-threatening illness, sensitizes the heart of the pilgrim to appreciate the presence of God in everyday people, in everyday thoughts, and in everyday events. Contrary to the traditional understanding of pilgrimage, God does not have to be sought. God seeks us. The final blessing of a pilgrimage is to understand that the God we have traveled so far to meet was with us all the time. We need only to open our minds and hearts to that truth.

This truth has never been more beautifully expressed as in the words of Jean-Pierre de Caussade:

"All you suffer, all you do, all your inclinations are mysteries under which God gives himself to you." [xcvi]

About the Author

Réjeanne Marie Taylor, BA, B.Ed., MA - Liturgy & Spirituality

"About the Author" sections rarely capture the spirit or essence of a person. We thought a lot about what to put here but felt a simple list of traditional life milestones to be completely inadequate to describe this remarkable woman.

Réjeanne Taylor, our mother, was strong, reserved, kind, and extraordinary. Above all, the two things most important to our mother were family and spirituality. Often the lines between them blurred as she was constantly exploring, learning, and growing. Looking back, Dad has described our childhood home as Mom's single-family Montessori preschool and it is that thirst for self-growth for all that has always been at her core. And although family always came first, good friends were also enveloped completely into her fold. Extended family gatherings have always been annual… and large. And Mom would inevitably be at the center of making sure the food (and wine) were organized and plentiful.

At the absolute core of family for Mom was our Dad and I've rarely seen as pure a moment of love as when my parents paused in the middle of whatever family chaos was happening to share a kiss.

Mom set aside her career and stayed home to raise our family of 3 young children. She organized innumerable trips tent camping with us as small children, and as we grew so did the family adventures: to her beloved Rocky Mountains, the West Coast Trail, and on a trip that changed all our lives when Mom decided we would walk the Camino de Santiago to celebrate their 25th wedding anniversary.

Mom's passion for learning caused her to question and to seek more. From delving into discussions about religion and its complicated relationship to individual spirituality, to deciding to complete a Master's degree in Liturgy & Spirituality, she was always searching for deeper understanding. Never content to take her faith as a given, she found peace in seeking and growing, reaching for a deeper, more refined meaning.

Shortly after Mom's first Camino, the pilgrimage model and the Labyrinth became ever present in our lives as tools of guidance, to help us find some understanding and peace in the various stages of our own life journeys. *Between the Stars and the Stones* is our Mom – sharing the pilgrimage model and her learnings with an even wider family, so that we can all reflect during the tough journeys and find companionship and peace along the dusty road.

Réjeanne's children (in order of appearance):

Nicole Salens
Dave Taylor
Danelle Prescesky

Resources

1. Based on her understanding of the stages of pilgrimage and the responses and actions that an individual might take during each of these stages, Réjeanne developed a chart that can help a pilgrim navigate those stages – whether for a physical pilgrimage or another tough life journey.

   To download a copy of this chart, go to our website: www.passionatepilgrim.ca

2. Réjeanne had developed other resources that she used in her workshops and in her own later cancer journeys. These, including templates for creating a Pilgrims Passport specific to your journey, will also be made available on our website.

3. Prior to her death, Réjeanne had developed most of a book of poems paralleling the stages of pilgrimage which will be published in due course.

   Look for *Stones Speak* in mid-2015 on www.passionatepilgrim.ca or on lulu.com

4. Tom Batiuk's book **"Lisa's Story: The Other Shoe"** (published September 2007) is a collection of both the 1999 comic strips on Lisa's initial battle with cancer and the later series examining her struggle with the disease and its outcome. Additionally, it contains resource material on breast cancer, including early detection, information sources, support systems, and health care. It can be purchased through Amazon.

End Note

Forward

[i] Rejeanne Taylor, *Perichoresis: The Mysterious Dance of Two Journeys – My Pilgrimage to Santiago de Compostela & My Pilgrimage with Breast Cancer* (Edmonton, AB: St. Stephen's College, 2000)

Introduction

[ii] Margaret Pawley, *Prayers for Pilgrims* (London: Society for Promoting Christian Knowledge, 1991) p.xiii
[iii] Thich Nhat Hanh, quoted in Cousineau, *The Art of Pilgrimage: The Seekers Guide to Making Travel Sacred* (Berkeley: Conan Press, 1998) 203
[iv] Cousineau, *Pilgrimage*

Chapter 1: Longing (Anticipation – Anxiety)

[v] Jim Cotter, *Prayer at Day's Dawning* (Sheffield: Cairns Publications, 1998) 157.
[vi] Martin Robinson, ed., *Sacred Places, Pilgrim Paths: An Anthology of Pilgrimage* (London: Harper Collins Publishers, 1997) 2.
[vii] Phil Cousineau, *The Art of Pilgrimage: The Seeker's Guide to Making Travel Sacred* (Berkeley: Conari Press, 1998) 15.
[viii] Henry David Thoreau, *Walden* (Columbus: Charles E. Merrill Publishing Company, 1969) 98.
[ix] Cousineau, *Pilgrimage* 181.
[x] Stephanie Byram, photography by Charlee Brodsky, *Cancer Destroys, Cancer Builds* <eng.hss.cmu.edu/Cultronix/stephanie> 1996, <.../PhotoEssay/photo.3.html>, accessed 13 October 1999.
[xi] Cousineau, *Pilgrimage* 18.
[xii] The term *initiate* is offered as an alternative to the identifier *survivor* in the work by Kuner, Matzkin Orsborn, Quigley, and Leigh Stroup, *Language of Healing* 15.
[xiii] Dat Nguyen, personal interview, 17 February 1999.

[xiv] Louise Rose, "Nobody Wants To Sing The Blues", c.d. *Changed* (Elar Ent., 1996).

[xv] David Goa, personal interview, 5 February 1999.

[xvi] McNamara, *Mystical Passion* 8.

[xvii] Paraphrased by Judith Cornell, *Mandala: Luminous Symbols for Healing* (Wheaton, Il: Quest Books, 1994) 26. For Paramahansa Yogananda's own words, see *Autobiography of a Yogi* (Los Angeles: Self-Realization Fellowship, 1999) 311.

Chapter 2: Call
(Excitement – Terror)

[xviii] As quoted by Deborah Cowley, "Along The Pilgrims' Path," *Reader's Digest* April 1996: 39.

[xix] As quoted by Cowley, "Pilgrims' Path" 42.

[xx] As quoted by Cowley, "Pilgrims' Path" 43.

[xxi] Herbert Anderson and Edward Foley, *Mighty Stories, Dangerous Rituals: Weaving Together the Human and the Divine* (San Francisco: Jossey-Bass Publishers, 1998) 53.

[xxii] Job 1:22, The Living Bible

[xxiii] Job 2:6

[xxiv] Brian Hebblethwaite, *Evil, Suffering and Religion* (London: Sheldon Press, 1976) 50.

[xxv] This is a paraphrase based on what I remember of the original message.

[xxvi] Matzkin Orsborn, *Language of Healing* 131.

[xxvii] John E. Packo, *Coping With Cancer and Other Chronic or Life-Threatening Diseases* (Camp Hill: Christian Publications, 1991) 37.

[xxviii] Susan M. Love, *Dr. Susan Love's Breast Book* (Don Mills, Ontario: Addison-Wesley Publishing Company, 1995) 181.

[xxix] Love, *Breast Book* 195-218.

[xxx] Love, *Breast Book* 182.

[xxxi] H. Seidman, S.D. Stellman, and M.H. Mushinski, "A different perspective on breast cancer risk factors: Some implications of the non-attributable risk," *CA: A Cancer "Journal" for Clinicians* (1982) 32:301, as cited in Love, *Breast Book* 182.

[xxxii] Isis was the most important female goddess of the ancient Egyptians. She was the mother of all things, the queen of all the elements, the beginning of all time. "Isis," *The World Book Encyclopedia*, 1985 ed. Underhill suggests here that hidden behind the veil of the creator goddess are all the mysteries of life.

[xxxiii] Evelyn Underhill, *Mysticism: A Study in the Nature and Development of Man's Spiritual Consciousness* (New York: The New American Library, Inc., 1974) 48.

[xxxiv] Salvador Andrés Ordax, *San Juan De Ortega: A Sanctuary On St. James' Way* (León: Edilesa , 1995)7.

[xxxv] Underhill, *Mysticism* 47.

[xxxvi] Jules Supervielle, "The Call", quoted in Cousineau, *Pilgrimage* 29.

[xxxvii] Since renovated and vastly improved.

[xxxviii] Kosuke Koyama, "Pilgrim or Tourist?" (Christians Conference of Asia, 1974) 1-3, as quoted in Robinson, *Sacred Places,* 49.

[xxxix] David N. Power, "Let the Sick Man Call," *The Heythrop* "Journal" 19 (1978) 256-270, quoted in "Sickness and Symbol: The Promise of the Future", Jennifer Glen, *Worship* 54 (1980) 397.

[xl] "Mindfulness is considered the heart of Buddhist meditation but its essence is universal and of deep practical benefit to all." Jon Kabat-Zinn, *Wherever You Go There You Are: Mindfulness Meditation In Everyday Life* (New York: Hyperion, 1994) front flap of cover.

[xli] Thoreau, *Walden* 105.

[xlii] McNamara, *Passion* 116.

[xliii] McNamara, *Passion* 116.

[xliv] Kabir, quoted in Brother David Steindl-Rast, *Gratefulness, The Heart of Prayer: An Approach to Life in Fullness* (Ramsay, N.J.: Paulist Press, 1984) 7.

Chapter 3: Preparation (Intention – Fate)

[xlv] Cousineau, *Pilgrimage* 77.

[xlvi] *Confraternity of St. James* <http://www.csj.org.uk> first accessed February 1997, later accessed 14 February 2000.

[xlvii] *Pilgrim Guides to Spain: 1. The Camino Francés 1997* (London: The Confraternity of St. James, 1997).

[xlviii] 'Pilgrimages', *New Catholic Encyclopedia* (1967) quoted in Robinson, *Sacred Places* 55.

[xlix] Jennifer Glen, "Sickness and Symbol: The Promise of the Future," *Worship* 54 (1980): 400.

[l] "Ductal Carcinoma in Situ of the Breast," *Annals of Internal Medicine* 1 December 1997, 127:1013-1022. <http://www.acponline.org/journals/annals/01dec97/ductal.htm>, accessed 10 December 1998.

[li] "Recent trends in the management of breast cancer. 1. Carcinoma in situ of the breast." *Can J Surg* (August 1992), 35(4):361-5.

<http://www.ncbi.nlm.nih.gov/htbin-post/Entrez/query?uid=1323379&form=6&db=m&Dopt=b>, accessed 10 December 1998.

[lii] Cousineau, *Pilgrimage* xxviii.
[liii] Lorde, *Journals* 68.
[liv] Lorde, *Journals* 9.
[lv] Anderson & Foley, *Mighty Stories* 7.
[lvi] Cousineau, *Pilgrimage* 63.
[lvii] Sir Walter Raleigh, "His Pilgrimage" <http://www.bartleby.com/101/77.html>, accessed 10 March 2000.
[lviii] Anderson & Foley, *Mighty Stories* 128.
[lix] Jonathan Sumption, *Pilgrimage: An Image of Medieval Religion* (1975), 170-1, quoted in Robinson, *Sacred Places* 54.
[lx] Trish O'Reilly, quoted in Cousineau, *Pilgrimage* 73.
[lxi] Cousineau, *Pilgrimage* xxviii.
[lxii] Mevlana Rumi, quoted in Cousineau, *Pilgrimage* xxviii.
[lxiii] Anderson & Foley, *Mighty Stories* 20.
[lxiv] *A Pilgrim Blessing*, trans. David Leo FSC (London: Confraternity of St. James, 1989) 3. The text in this pamphlet is a translation of a French version of the original Latin text of a medieval rite, dated 1078, preserved in the Missal of Vich Cathedral, Barcelona, Spain.

Chapter 4: Journey (Perseverance – Helplessness)

[lxv] Brother Ramon SSF, *The Heart of Prayer* (1995) 132, quoted in Robinson, *Sacred Places* 145.
[lxvi] David Taylor, "The Road to Santiago: journal of a modern pilgrim", 31 August 1997.
[lxvii] Robinson, *Sacred Places* 84.
[lxviii] Danelle Taylor, "The Road to Santiago: journal of a modern pilgrim", 4 September 1997.
[lxix] Nicole Taylor, "The Road to Santiago: journal of a modern pilgrim", 31 August 1997.
[lxx] Réjeanne Taylor, unpublished poem, March 2000
[lxxi] Antonio Machado, quoted in Cousineau, *Pilgrimage* xxx.
[lxxii] "Mutt and Jeff," cartoon strip launched in 1908 by sports cartoonist, Bud Fisher. This strip followed the antics of a lanky, horse-playing schemer named Augustus Mutt and his good-hearted shorter friend, Jeff. "Eeek! Gasp! Wow! 100 Years of Comics" by Eugene J. Walter, Jr., *The World Book Encyclopedia Year Book* 1996, 152.

[lxxiii] Réjeanne Taylor, unpublished poem, March 2000
[lxxiv] Laurie Dennett, "To Be a Pilgrim," *The Confraternity of St. James Bulletin no.59* May 1997, 2. <http://www.csj.org.uk/spirit.htm>, accessed 16 March 2000.
[lxxv] Lupe Rodriguez, "Pilgrim's Progress: Walking the Way of St. James", printed in one of the two1999 newsletters of The Little Company of Pilgrims, Mississauga. This article was reproduced in the newsletter with her permission from a publication of the Kitchener-Waterloo Art Gallery.
[lxxvi] David Taylor, "Journal", 31 August 1997.
[lxxvii] Danelle Taylor, "Journal", 1 September 1997.
[lxxviii] Nicole Taylor, "Journal", 6 September 1997.
[lxxix] Réjeanne had left a note in her manuscript "Add a few words about the characters of the camino..." Bob, her husband and co-pilgrim, added this paragraph.
[lxxx] Lorde, *Journals* 55.
[lxxxi] Réjeanne Taylor, from unpublished poem, "Walking".
[lxxxii] Holt, *Thirsty for God* 66.
[lxxxiii] John Bunyan, *The Pilgrim's Progress* (1678), quoted in Robinson, *Sacred Places* 187.
[lxxxiv] Réjeanne had left a note in her manuscript: "Here, write about the let-down regarding having come to the end of the road". Bob, her husband and co-pilgrim, has attempted to capture the essence of a topic they had discussed at length.

[lxxxv] Father Stephen Canny, as quoted in Cousineau, *Pilgrimage* 173.
[lxxxvi] Norvene Vest, *Friend of the Soul: A Benedictine Spirituality of Work* (Cambridge: Cowley Publications, 1997) 92.

Chapter 5: Arrival & Return
(Compassion – Self-Interest)

[lxxxvii] Hermann Künig von Vach, "The Pilgrim's Notebook of Hermann Künig von Vach," quoted in Millán Bravo Lozano, *A Practical Guide For Pilgrims: The Road To Santiago* (León: Editorial Everest, S.A., 1993) 240.
[lxxxviii] The Jesse Tree is a genealogical tree of Jesus beginning with Jesse, father of David. José Guerra Campos and Jesús Precedo Lafuente, *Guide To The Cathedral of Santiago de Compostela* (Vitoria, Spain: Aldeasa, 1997) 58.
[lxxxix] David Taylor, unpublished poem [Note that by reading down the first letter of each line and then down the last letter of each line, one reads the words: The art of pain].

[xc] Lorde, *Journals* 37.

[xci] In retrospect, I should have fabricated a *credential* for this pilgrimage and located "stamps" to mark the completion of various steps of this journey. And perhaps, like on the Camino, I could have made a personal journal to record my daily experiences, impressions, thoughts, feelings and insights. In s subsequent cancer journey, Réjeanne did create both the steps of her journey and her "virtual walking pilgrimage during treatment – both of which were immensely helpful. See "Resources"

[xcii] Bob Taylor, "The Road to Santiago: journal of a modern pilgrim", 26 September 1997.

Chapter 6: Blessings
(Wholeness – Infirmity)

[xciii] "Prayer of a French pilgrim", 27 September 1997, Cathedral of Santiago de Compostela, Spain, trans. Réjeanne Taylor.

[xciv] Tom Batiuk, *Funky Winkerbean: Lisa's Breast Cancer Story* <http://www.funkywinkerbean.com> Used with permission.

[xcv] John Bunyan, *The Pilgrim's Progress* [1678] <http://ccel.org/b/bunyan/pilgrims_progress/pilgrim1.html>, accessed 3 April 2000.

[xcvi] Jean-Pierre de Caussade, *Abandonment to Divine Providence*, trans. John Beevers (Toronto: Image Books, Doubleday, 1975) 96.